DISC

FINSICH

D0727808

EXPLORE

LISBON

NPLF

Nashville Public Library | FOUNDATION

*This book added
to the library's collection
through the generosity of the
the Joyce Family Foundation*

NPLF.ORG

◉ Walking Eye App

YOUR FREE EBOOK AVAILABLE THROUGH THE WALKING EYE APP

Your guide now includes a free eBook to your chosen destination, for the same great price as before. Simply download the Walking Eye App from the App Store or Google Play to access your free eBook.

HOW THE WALKING EYE APP WORKS

Through the Walking Eye App, you can purchase a range of eBooks and destination content. However, when you buy this book, you can download the corresponding eBook for free. Just see below in the grey panel where to find your free content and then scan the QR code at the bottom of this page.

Destinations: Download essential destination content featuring recommended sights and attractions, restaurants, hotels and an A–Z of practical information, all available for purchase.

Ships: Interested in ship reviews? Find independent reviews of river and ocean ships in this section, all available for purchase.

eBooks: You can download your free accompanying digital version of this guide here. You will also find a whole range of other eBooks, all available for purchase.

Free access to travel-related blog articles about different destinations, updated on a daily basis.

HOW THE EBOOKS WORK

The eBooks are provided in EPUB file format. Please note that you will need an eBook reader installed on your device to open the file. Many devices come with this as standard, but you may still need to install one manually from Google Play.

The eBook content is identical to the content in the printed guide.

HOW TO DOWNLOAD THE WALKING EYE APP

1. Download the Walking Eye App from the App Store or Google Play.
2. Open the app and select the scanning function from the main menu.
3. Scan the QR code on this page – you will then be asked a security question to verify ownership of the book.
4. Once this has been verified, you will see your eBook in the purchased ebook section, where you will be able to download it.

Other destination apps and eBooks are available for purchase separately or are free with the purchase of the Insight Guide book.

CONTENTS

ART BUFFS

Don't miss the treasures in the Gulbenkian (route 4), the masterpieces in the Museu Nacional de Arte Antiga (route 5) and the modern and contemporary art at the Museu Coleção Berardo (route 6).

RECOMMENDED ROUTES FOR...

CASTLES AND PALACES

Explore Lisbon's Castelo de São Jorge (route 1), visit the palaces of Mafra and Queluz (routes 13 and 14), or the Moorish castle ruins and fantasy palaces of Sintra (route 10).

FANS OF THE MANUELINE

Hop on a tram to Belém to see the famous monuments of the Mosteiro dos Jerónimos Monastery and Torre de Belém (route 6); and if in Setúbal (route 12), don't miss the remarkable Convento de Jesus.

FOODIES

Good restaurants are popping up all around the city but for some of the most memorable dining experiences, try the family-run *tascas* in the back alleys of Bairro Alto (route 3) or Alfama (route 1).

NIGHT OWLS

Join the revellers in bohemian Bairro Alto (route 3) or party the night away in trendy Cais do Sodré (Route 2). For *fado* head for the Alfama (route 1).

SHOPPERS

Explore the streets of Baixa (route 2) for quirky, old-fashioned stores, Chiado (route 3) for smart Art Deco shops and Bairro Alto (also route 3) for vintage chic and the latest trends.

TRAVELLING WITH CHILDREN

Europe's second largest Oceanarium (route 7) should be top of the agenda. Climb up and down hills on the rattling Tram 28 (route 9), cross the river to the Cristo Rei (route 8) or have fun on the beach (route 11).

VIEWS

For dazzling city and river views head up to the *miradouros* (viewpoints) such as the Castle Belvedere, Portas do Sol, Miradouro da Santa Luzia (route 1) or Miradouro de São Pedro de Alcântara (route 3).

INTRODUCTION

An introduction to Lisbon's geography, customs and culture, plus illuminating background information on cuisine, history and what to do when you're there.

See Lisbon's most famous sights by tram

EXPLORE LISBON

With its sunny climate, rich history and old world charm, Lisbon has an enduring appeal. Add gastronomy, nightlife and affordable prices and it is little wonder the Portuguese capital has become one of Europe's tourist hotspots.

Located on the broad estuary of the River Tagus where it spills into the Atlantic, Lisbon is Europe's most westerly capital. The city's waterfront forms an arc stretching nearly 32km (21 miles) along the river. Towards the Atlantic is Belém, launching point for Vasco da Gama and other explorers of the Age of Discovery, and at the eastern extreme is the Parque das Nações, site of Expo '98 and the face of 21st century Lisbon. Between the two is central Lisbon: the kasbah-like Alfama topped by the Moorish castle, the quintessential hilltop Bairro Alto and in the middle, downtown Baixa, elegantly rebuilt in the 18th century after one of the worst earthquakes ever recorded.

GEOGRAPHY AND LAYOUT

Much of Lisbon's appeal lies in its location. Water is omnipresent. Set on seven hills, the city offers myriad *miradouros* (look-out points) which afford spectacular views over terracotta roof tiles to the placid Tagus. Two of the largest bridges in Europe reach across the estuary, an expanse of water which is so wide it gives a sense of the sea. Just past the district of Belém, where Manueline monuments stands as symbols of Portugal's Golden Age, a lighthouse marks the point where the river ends and the Atlantic begins. The ocean defines the city: its limpid light turns to gold – a 'Straw Sea' – in the afternoon sun.

Any city map shows that many of the top attractions of the city are within walking distance of the river, but because of the hills and the way in which the sights are spread out, it isn't always easy to go directly from one to another. Locals carry bags of bread and groceries up and down Lisbon's hills without complaint, even in mid-summer, and tourists who wander on foot are rewarded with picturesque nooks or brilliant panoramas. Public transport, however, is cheap and, most of the time, efficient. Vintage trams rattle their way around the old town; funiculars make light work of steep hills; the metro is modern and fast; buses straightforward; and taxis plentiful and inexpensive.

The routes in the guide first explore the diverse neighbourhoods of the city centre, then focus on outlying areas, particularly Belém, whose Manueline monuments are symbols of Portugal's

Tiles in Restauradores metro

Local shops in Baixa

late 15th century Golden Age. But quaint neighbourhoods, a beautiful cityscape and monuments to former splendour are not the end of the capital's charms. Lisbon is surrounded by some of Portugal's most appealing spots, most of them easily reached by public transport. For visitors with time to venture beyond the city, there are trips to magical Sintra, with palaces and *quintas* (estates) studding beautiful pine-clad hills, or west to the sparkling beach resorts of the Cascais coast and the Atlantic-battered beaches to the north, while over the Tagus to the south those with a car can explore the wild Serra da Arrábida. To the north lies the monumental palace-convent of Mafra; closer to the capital, the handsome Versailles-style palace at Queluz is another major draw for visitors, including heads of state.

CLIMATE

Although the cold Atlantic lies only a few kilometres downriver, Lisbon feels decidedly Mediterranean. A sheltered, south-facing location and mild winters allow palm trees and bird-of-paradise flowers to flourish, and the balmy weather encourages an unhurried pace. It is a year-round destination but the best times to visit the city are spring and autumn, when temperatures are pleasant, there are fewer crowds than summer and plenty of cultural activities to keep you busy. May and October are ideal. Summers can be very hot but you can always cool off on nearby beaches to the west and south of the capital. Temperatures normally remain warm until November and even in winter it can still be mild, with plenty of sunny days.

POPULATION

The biggest city in Portugal, Lisbon is home to a population of around 550,000 people in the centre, with over 3 million

The Great Earthquake

On 1st November 1755 a massive earthquake shook the whole of Europe, and ripped through the city of Lisbon. It was All Saints' Day and churches were packed with crowds. Buildings crumbled, fires spread and the waters of the Tagus heaved into a tidal wave which steamrollered the port and lower town with devastating force. The triple disaster is estimated to have killed between 15,000 and 60,000 of the 270,000 residents. 'Nothing was left' a witness wrote, 'but desolation and sorrow'. Yet Lisbon grew again in grace and stature under the guiding hand of the already powerful Marquês de Pombal, Chief Minister to the ineffective and profligate King José I. His methods were tough, ambitious and tyrannical but in the following 20 years or so he masterminded Portugal's reconstruction from the ruins. The neoclassical architectural style of the Baixa was rapidly dubbed 'pombalina'.

Taking in the view from Miradouro de Santa Luzia

throughout greater Lisbon – making up about half of Portugal's total population. In spite of the inescapable presence of a greater past, this is a modern, cosmopolitan capital, which has a sense of the world outside. The city's streets teem with people of diverse ethnicity and dress. Many are migrants from Portugal's former African colonies: Angola, Cape Verde, Mozambique, or from Brazil, Macau and Goa, who arrived in Lisbon and soon founded their own little colonies, speaking a slightly softer version of the language and adding spice to the cuisine.

The Golden Age

Lisbon's gaze was always fixed firmly out to sea. Once a remote outpost of what was thought to be the farthest edge of the known world, by the 15th century the town had become the centre of Portuguese exploration. It was from Lisbon that Vasco da Gama set out on his sea voyage in the summer of 1497, on the sea route to the spices of the East. Reaching Calicut in southern India the following year, Portugal put an end to the Venetian monopoly of the Eastern spice trade by assuming control of the Indian Ocean and attracting merchants from all over Europe to Lisbon. Further territories were discovered when Pedro Álvares Cabral reached Brazil in 1500 and Lisbon was converted from a European backwater into a wealthy world city. Even after the catastrophic earthquake of 1755, no expense was spared in re-planning and rebuilding. As Lisbon is one of the few European capitals to have survived the continent's 20th-century wars unscathed, many of the historic buildings remain intact, an enduring testimony to a prosperous and glorious past.

LOCAL CUSTOMS

Through the centuries this cosmopolitan city has offered shelter to Europe's outcasts, becoming a haven for exiles and a last refuge to monarchs who had lost their thrones. Today, Lisbon continues its tradition of extending a warm welcome to visitors. And of all Portugal's friends, none have endured as long as the English. The Anglo-Portuguese Alliance, ratifed at the Treaty of Windsor in 1386, is the longest continuing alliance in world history. An increasing number of Lisboetas speak good English, particularly those who work in tourist-facing jobs. You are unlikely to have any problem being understood in hotels and restaurants, but if you do master a few words of Portuguese, the effort will always be appreciated.

Eating out in the city is a way of life. The Portuguese love their food, and one of the great joys of visiting Lisbon is the food and wine on offer, whether they are enjoyed at a family-run *tasca*, beachside taverna or one of the capital's chic designer restaurants and bars. Local

The Ponte 25 de Abril

cooking owes much to Portugal's close ties to the sea. Fresh fish and seafood are abundant, and served in almost every restaurant.

If you want buzz by night – and there is plenty of it – start the evening late. Many restaurants don't come to life until around 9pm and it's around this time that the powerful and soulful strains of *fado* beckon from the streets of Bairro Alto or Alfama. Meanwhile, Lisbon's bars and clubs offer a great night out until the early hours.

LOCAL ECONOMY

Once the poorest EU country in Western Europe, Lisbon has benefitted hugely from EU investment. The new millennium has seen an altered, enlarged and

---

DON'T LEAVE LISBON WITHOUT......

Reaching the dizzy heights. Take a lift, a tram or shanks' pony to one of Lisbon's many *miradouros* (belvederes) for unforgettable views of the city and river.

Sampling custard tarts (*pastéis de nata*). Discover these culinary delights at virtually any café, bakery or *pasteleria*, but ideally at Pastéis de Belém which sells well over 10,000 a day, warm from the oven. See page 16.

Taking a trip on Tram 28. Hop on the No 28 vintage tram and enjoy views of Lisbon's iconic landmarks as it rattles up and down the hills. See page 74.

Try *bacalhau*. It might not sound great, but the Portuguese do some delicious dishes with this salted, dried cod. There are said to be 365 recipes – one for every day of the year. Try it in one of the family restaurants in the backstreets of Alfama. See page 18.

Bar-hopping in the Bairro Alto. Sleepy by day, the Bairro Alto buzzes by night. By around 11pm, the bar-lined streets here take on a carnival street-party vibe. Follow the flow and discover countless bars and nightclubs, some open until 5am. See page 47.

Time Out Mercado da Ribeira. This hugely successful haven for gourmets has 35 kiosks serving cuisine from leading Portuguese chefs. Whatever Portuguese (and beyond) speciality you want to try, this is the place to come. See page 117.

Experiencing Fado. Listen to *fado*, Portugal's musical expression of longing and sorrow. Many places offer an evening of *fado* with food and wine. See page 23.

Back alleys of Alfama. Explore the labyrinthine backstreets of Moorish Alfama, which retains a village-like atmosphere. See page 28.

Taking a break by the sea. Leave the bustle of the city behind, hop on a train and head for the Cascais coast for the cooling Atlantic breeze. See page 85.

A cherry fix. Join the locals in the Largo de São Domingos quarter at one of the little *ginjinha* bars. A shot of this sweet cherry liqueur comes with or without cherries and costs little more than a euro. See page 40.

dynamic city. As hosts of Expo '98, the world fair held on the 500th anniversary of Vasco da Gama's discovery of the sea route to India, Lisbon launched a brand new neighbourhood, the Parque das Nações. A derelict industrial site was revitalised into a high-tech site of futuristic buildings, a giant oceanarium and over the Tagus, the gleaming 17km (10.6 mile) Ponte de Vasco da Gama, the longest bridge in Europe.

Ten years on, the financial crisis of 2008 left Portugal with a budget deficit that was fast spiralling out of control. In 2011 it became the third EU country after Greece and Ireland to ask for a financial bail-out (€78 bn) from the EU. It wasn't until 2014, after harsh austerity measures that had been implemented and the budget deficit reduced, that Portugal exited the bailout programme. Since 2014, the country has been on a slow economic recovery path.

The economy is based primarily on industry and services. Tourism accounts for at least 10 per cent of Portugal's GDP, helping to boost economic figures. Lisbon now sees nearly 3.6 million foreign visitors annually, an increase of over 32 percent on visitor numbers three years ago. The climate and the affordable prices are two of the main factors – it is one of the cheapest cities in western Europe. Lisbon has also become a popular stop for cruise ships. Recent years have seen a boom in new hotels and restaurants; while crumbling buildings in the centre, abandoned for

years, are starting to be snapped up by foreign Europeans attracted by Portugal's tax-friendly non-habitual residents (NHR) programme – or for conversion by locals to new cafés, bars or small businesses.

LISBON TODAY

Lisbon's contemporary culture is thriving. Former no-go areas have become hip neighbourhoods, with urban art, cool boutiques and galleries promoting all things Portuguese. The latest cultural hub is MAAT, the Museum for Art, Architecture and Technology bordering the Tagus in Belém and resembling a sleek, gentle wave. This and other attractions on the Lisbon waterside are part of the revival of the city's historic link with the river and the sea which began in the late 20th century. Old quays and warehouses have been transformed, becoming a lively focus of activity by day and night. The latest development is the waterfront west of the main Praça do Comércio, now an inviting promenade for strolling, cycling or just sitting on a deckchair watching boats go by.

Lisbon has seen a dramatic and fast transformation, emerging as one of Europe's most dynamic capitals. At the same time, it still has the feel of a laid-back provincial capital, known above all for the charms of its narrow Moorish-style streets, the beauty of its hand-painted *azulejos* (tiles) and the occasional ornate architectural flour-

Lisbon's hills surveyed from Sao Pedro de Alcantara

ish. Historic village-like neighbourhoods retain their quirky appeal, vintage trams still rattle up and down its steep hills, washing flaps on crumbling facades and old timers still enjoy a *bica* or a tot of *ginginja* in the many old cafés and bars. Lisbon has changed with the times but its old-world charm is never far away.

TOP TIPS FOR VISITING LISBON

Tickets. Good value, particularly for sightseers, is the Lisboa Card, available from tourist offices for one, two or three days. It entitles you to free metro, bus, tram and lift transport, admission to over 20 sights (including some outside Lisbon) plus special offers in restaurants, shops and other venues. The card is available for 24, 48 and 72 hours and costs €18.50, €31.50 and €39 respectively. Remember that most museums close on Mondays.

Free appetisers. Most restaurants serve unrequested appetisers such as bread, butter, olives, cheese and fish pâtés that appear to be free. They are not. You will be charged a few euros for these, but you have the option (if you're strong-willed!) to leave them untouched and not be charged.

Market price. If you see *'preco V'* (or simply *'PV'*) beside the seafood on a menu, it means the price is variable depending on the day's market price. Ask the price before ordering.

Cheap eats. To fill up for a few euros, opt for the *ementa turística*, a daily-changing set menu, including coffee and a drink. The *prato do dia* is the dish of the day, often a good choice.

Musical offerings. Keep your ears open for concerts as you stroll around and your eyes open for posters and flyers advertising them.

Look out for free concerts, eg at Palácio Foz and the Gulbenkian Museum, and open-air ones in the city from June to September.

Reserve a table. As the best eateries are often both cramped and coveted by Lisboetas, call at least a day in advance to assure yourself a table. At weekends this is essential.

Shopping Card. The Lisboa Shopping Card offers discounts from five to 15 percent in Baixa, Chiado and the Avenida da Liberdade. The card is available in a one- or two-day version (€3.70 or €5.80) from the airport or any tourist office.

Tram tips. Lisbon's loveable trams are packed with tourists. To ensure a seat take the tram from its departure point rather than trying to alight half way along the route.

The price of people-watching. An increasing number of cafés, particularly those in the famous squares, have started charging extra for table service. But in neighbourhood cafés and bars you still pay the same whether it's a drink at the bar or on the terrace.

Visiting for free. The top free sight is the Museu Coleção Berardo in Belém, a fabulous collection of modern and contemporary art. Some museums are free on the first Sunday of the month. For free 3-hour walking tours visit www.neweuropetours.eu.

Try porco à Alentejana

FOOD AND DRINK

Choose from trusty hole-in-the-wall tascas, riverside or beach seafood restaurants, retro bistros or new culinary hotspots where creative chefs have given Portuguese cuisine a contemporary twist.

Local food is usually fresh, filling and full of flavour; and if you avoid the tourist traps you can eat well and cheaply. The Lisbon dining scene has become much more diverse in recent years and the city is fast becoming one of Europe's most fashionable culinary capitals.

With its river setting and proximity to the sea the city has a wonderful abundance of fish and seafood. Visit any fish market and you will see a gleaming array of squid (*lula*), cuttlefish (*choco*), octopus (*polvo*) sea bass (*robalo*), gilthead bream (*dourada*), sardines (*sardinhas*) and shellfish such as oysters (*ostras*), clams (*ameijoas*) and lobster (*lagosta*).

Flavours from China, India, Brazil and Africa reflect Portugal's colonial past. The former colony of Goa accounts for the local popularity of *caril* (curry) and other Indian-style dishes. *Piri-piri*, often served with chicken, is a hot chilli sauce from Angola that will set most mouths ablaze. Four centuries of ties with Macau assures all lovers of Chinese food a night out with dishes such as *gambas doces* (sweet-and-sour prawns).

Secret tarts

You can't go to Lisbon and not sample the *pastéis de Belém*, creamy custard tarts made to a special and, of course, secret recipe. The tarts, generically known as *pastéis de nata*, can be found all over the city but those from the Pastéis de Belém (see page 66) are the crème de la crème. The story goes that they used to be made by the monks of the Jerónimos Monastery, just a few steps away, and that when the monasteries were dissolved in the 1830s the recipe was passed on to a local baker. It is also said that only three bakers at any one time know the recipe, which they pass on to someone else on retirement.

PLACES TO EAT

Tascas which are typically found in the narrow streets of Baixa, Alfama and Bairro Alto, are traditionally tiny, family-run joints serving hearty helpings of authentic Portuguese cuisine. Some have seen a modern makeover in recent years but are still faithful to local fare. A *churrasqueira* is a grill, typically very simple with paper tablecloths, serving fare like grilled sardines or half

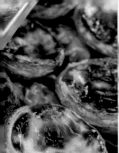

Pastéis de Belém

Portuguese cheese

chickens. A *marisqueira* will specialise in seafood, a *cervejaria* is a beer house, but normally serves seafood and steaks as well as a good choice of beer. A *restaurante* is used for a whole range of eateries, from sumptuous to basic. The tourist menu *(ementa turística)* offered by some restaurants, particularly at lunchtime, changes daily and can be excellent value. Lisbon has a vibrant *café* culture, with a staggering number of places offering the simple pleasure of relaxing over a cup of good coffee and a freshly-made pastry. Dotted around the city are dark green *kiosks* offering snacks and drinks at reasonable prices, some sited on hills with wonderful views. For markets see Restaurants, page 116.

WHAT TO EAT

No sooner are you seated than pre-starters of bread, butter, cheese and maybe olives, fish pâté or slices of cured ham will appear on the table. These are optional temptations and there is nearly always a charge. It may only be a euro or two for bread or olives, but it could be €5 for the cheese or meat. If you don't touch them you won't be charged.

Soups and starters
Starters are typically seafood (see below), speciality hams and cheeses or hale-and-hearty soups. *Caldo verde*, a kale and potato soup, sometimes with sausage added, is served from the classiest restaurant to the humblest *tasca*. *Sopa à Portuguesa* is similar to *caldo verde* but with added broccoli, turnips, beans, carrots and anything else the cook happens to have to hand. Thick bread soups include *açorda à Alentejana* with coriander, garlic and whole poached eggs, and *açorda de marisco*, a spicy, garlicky shellfish broth. Other starters are cured and smoked hams, or sausages and salamis, often heavily smoked and spiced.

Fish and seafood
Seafood restaurants often sell shellfish by the weight, giving the price in euros per kilo. A number of seafood dishes are true local specialities. *Caldeirada de peixe* is a rich seafood stew; *arroz de marisco* is a delicious seafood rice dish with crab, lobster claws, prawns, clams and cockles; *ameijoas na cataplana* is steamed clams with chorizo or another type of pork with tomato, white wine, ham, onion and herbs. Clams are often served simply with crushed garlic cloves and fresh coriander: *amêijoas à bulhão pato*. If you like squid, try them stuffed with rice, olives, tomato onion and herb *(lulas recheadas)*, though the large squid are often grilled and served on a skewer *(espetada)* with prawns *(gambas)*. Fish dishes normally come simply grilled. You can't tell from the menu whether it's fresh or frozen, so ask the waiter for the catch of the day. And don't assume the bass and bream is from the high seas – much of it is farmed these days.

Simply–served, plump prawns with a glass of sparkling wine

The national dish

The Portuguese passion for *bacalhau*, dried salt-cod, fished in distant seas, may seem strange in a city on a river and close to the sea with so much fresh fish available. But you come across it every-where and the Portuguese claim to have 365 ways of preparing it, one for every day of the year. There are many savoury variations, such as *bacalhau à Gomes de Sá* (casseroled with potato, onion and olives) or *à brás* (flaked cod with fried potatoes, onions, eggs, parsley and topped with black olives) and such dishes make this local staple well worth sampling. If you just want a taste, try one of the *pastéis de bacalhau*, delicious lit-tle salt-cod croquettes, which are sold everywhere. With *bacalhau*, it's usual to drink red rather than white wine.

Meat dishes

Although fish and seafood predominate on menus and is the best thing to try, res-taurants do not skimp on meat. You can find excellent pork dishes, often roasted or served in robust stews, as well as chicken, steak, braised rabbit and wild boar. Be sure to try *porco à Alentejana*, pork and clams spiced with paprika. *Fei-joada*, a hearty stew of white beans, vege-tables and meat, usually includes pork of some sort, typically pigs' trotters and sau-sage. If you want to splash out, try the deli-cious *leitão assado* (roast suckling pig) served in the more expensive restaurants.

Chicken *(frango)* is popular and pre-pared in many ways but most commonly found as *frango piri-piri*, when it is mari-naded and barbecued to a tasty crisp with chilli oil. *Bife à café* is beef in a creamy sauce of milk, mustard and lemon juice, *pregas* are small steak sandwiches.

From April to September you'll see restaurants displaying signs saying 'Há Caracóis' where locals will be tucking into a platter of tiny snails, a local favourite, washed down with icy Sagres.

Desserts

The Portuguese have a sweet tooth and Lisbon is packed with *pastelerias* (patisse-ries), bakeries and cafés selling delicious cakes and pastries. The favourites are the *pastéis de nata* (custard tarts) eaten with coffee any time of day or as a dessert in almost every restaurant and café (see box, page 16). Other options are *pudim flan*, the Portuguese version of crème caramel, *arroz doce,* a lemon-flavoured rice pud-ding sprinkled with cinnamon and *pudim Molotov* which will explode any diet – the fluffy egg-white mousse is immersed in a sticky caramel sauce. You may also come across so-called 'convent sweets', as they

---

Food and drink prices

Throughout this book, the price categories for a two-course meal for one with a glass of house wine are:

€€€€ = over 40 euros
€€€ = 35–40 euros
€€ = 20–35 euros
€ = up to 20 euros

Fresh dourada for sale at the Mercado da Ribeira

were made by nuns in the 18th century to raise money. One of the more readily available is *Toucinho do Ceu*, 'food from heaven', made from sugar, almonds and egg yolks.

Cheese

If you still have space after dessert sample some Portuguese cheese. The richest and most expensive is *Serra da Estrela*, made from cured ewe's milk cheese which originates high up in the mountains and can be served fresh or cured. Some restaurants serve *queijo fresco* (fresh cheese) as an appetiser. This is usually a small, white, soft cheese made of ewe's and goat's milk, but it's fairly bland so you may want to season it.

Wine

Portuguese table wine has come on in leaps and bounds in recent years. Try the Alentejo wines, available everywhere in Lisbon. The region produces high-quality reds and an increasing number of good whites, all very reasonably priced. The Dão region produces some of the country's finest red wines, as does the Douro Valley, traditionally best known for port.

Vinho verde (green wine) is a refreshing, slightly sparkling young wine, which goes well with seafood.

Fortified port wine has tantalised palates around the world since the British began exporting it in the 17th century. The best place in Lisbon to sample the famous port wines is the Solar do Vinho do Porto (see page 44) Port and Madeira,

the two most celebrated Portuguese wines, are mostly known as postprandial dessert wines but may also be sipped as aperitifs. The before-dinner varieties are dry and extra-dry white port and the dry Madeiras, *Sercial* and *Verdelho.* These should be served slightly chilled. After dinner, sip one of the famous tawny ports (the aged varieties are especially good), or a Madeira dessert wine, *Boal* or *Malvasia* (also known as Malmsey).

Other drinks

Portuguese beers are good and refreshing. Light or dark, they are served chilled, bottled or from the tap. One of the best and most common brands is Sagres.

A favourite Portuguese tipple is *Ginjinha* (or *Ginja*), a sweet and potent cherry liqueur, which comes with or without cherries. It originated in Lisbon and you'll find it in all the bars, but most characteristically in the small *Ginjinha* bars around Rossio. The A Ginjinha bar on Rossio dates from 1840 and does a roaring trade all day and evening in cheap shots of the liqueur. It was once seen as a miracle cure for all manner of illnesses (and it may remind you of cough medicine).

Coffee

Coffee is a way of life for the Portuguese. The most popular form is *uma bica, a* small, stong espresso; a weaker version of is a *carioca*, with a drop of milk is a *garoto*. If you want plenty of milk with your coffee ask for a *galão* which comes small *(pequeno)* or tall *(grande).*

Folksy earthenware

SHOPPING

In Lisbon, young designers showing off their latest creations rub shoulders with old-fashioned stores that appear to have hardly altered in 100 years. Seek out Portuguese handicrafts, explore quirky vintage stores or pick up culinary treats.

Where to start a shopping trip? The Chiado district is the place to go for vintage clothes, jewellery, smart designer wear and interior design. It is home to the swish Armazéns do Chiado multi-level shopping centre and the elegant cafés and stores lining Rua Garrett, including the Bertrand bookshop, dating back to 1732.

For antique shops, hip boutiques and cutting edge designers head to the neighbouring Príncipe Real quarter. Embaixada (www.embaixadalx.pt) is a spectacular 19th century neo-Arab palace, converted into a hip shopping gallery focusing on avant-garde Portuguese design, craftsmanship, fashion and culture.

The central grid of streets around Rua Augusta in the Baixa contains some wonderfully atmospheric shops. Traditional foodstuffs, clothing and jewellery are all sold here, though Rua Augusta itself has a number of high-street chains.

MADE IN PORTUGAL

Portugal is famous for pottery and ceramics, found in many designs and colours from folksy earthenware to *azulejos*, the hand-painted decorative tiles and Vista Alegre fine porcelain tableware. For high quality hand-made tiles and ceramics using traditional techniques head to the Sant'Anna factory (www.santanna.com.pt) at Belém or their show room in Chiado. Also in Chiado, A Vida Portuguesa (www.avidaportuguesa.com) is a wonderful late 19th century emporium with genuine Portuguese products from retro-wrapped gourmet products to soaps, sprays, jewellery and notebooks. The large Lisbon Shop, at Rua do Arsenal 7-15 in the city centre, specialises in all things Portuguese and is an ideal store for affordable souvenirs.

Portugal produces over half the world's cork in terms of the raw material, more in

LX Factory

In Alcântara, the cool and creative LX Factory (Rua Rodrigues Faria 103, www.lxfactory.com) below the Ponte 25 Abril is a former industrial estate converted into workshops, art and design studios, boutiques, cafés and restaurants. A lively programme of events includes exhibitions, music, films – and a flea market on Sunday from noon to 7pm.

Rooster souvenirs   *Finds at the Feira da Ladra*

terms of the finished product. While more and more wine bottlers are using screw caps, new uses are being found for eco-friendly Portuguese cork. You can find finely crafted bags, lampshades, hats and handbags – all in cork. Try Cork & Co (www.corkandcompany.pt) in Bairro Alto.

GASTRONOMY

Groceries and delicatessens have a tempting array of smoked meats, whole hams, spicy sausages and cheeses. Manuel Tavares between Rossio and Praça da Figueira is one of Lisbon's oldest delis, offering fine wines and port, charcuterie, cheese and chocolates. The Conserveira de Lisboa (www.conserveira delisboa.pt) in Baixa is a lovely old-fashioned shop with attractively packaged gourmet fish (tinned tuna, squid, sardines etc). Portugal has long been famous for its fortified port wine from the Douro Valley near Oporto in the north. At the Solar do Vinho do Porto (see page 44) you can try before buying.

MARKETS

Markets are as fun for their ambience as much as the goods on offer. In the Campo de Santa Clara, the Feira da Ladra (Thieves' Market) is held on Tuesday and Saturday from dawn to dusk. This flea market has a large range of second-hand items and the very occasional dusty treasure. The Mercado da Ribeira at Cais do Sodré has a morning food market but the main tourist attraction is the buzzing food court, with over 30 gastronomic stalls presenting food from Portuguese top chefs. West of the centre, with less tourists, is the excellent Mercado de Campo Ourique, a traditional food market with a gourmet food hall.

HIGH-END DESIGN

A number of high-fashion designers from Portugal have gained international attention, and Chiado and Bairro Alto are good places to seek them out. The Portuguese leather industry is known throughout the world and jackets, belts, bags, wallets and shoes are popular and good-value buys. Over the last five years Lisbon has seen a fast growth in the luxury market. Big designer names such as Louis Vuitton, Gucci and Prada are almost all located on the Avenida da Liberdade.

SHOPPING CENTRES

The postmodern smoky glass towers of Amoreiras (www.amoreiras.com) house supermarkets, cinemas, art galleries and a food court as well as 200 stores, and (for a fee) great views from the top. Centro Colombo (www.colombo.pt) is the largest shopping centre in the Iberian Peninsula with over 340 stores, more akin to a massive leisure complex than a shopping mall. The mega Spanish department store El Corte Ingles (www.elcorteingles.pt) has 13 floors with everything from top designers to a huge supermarket.

Fado in Bairro Alto

ENTERTAINMENT

The Portuguese capital is a great place to party, with venues ranging from fado speakeasies to super-clubs, and from African nightclubs to alternative bars. Lisbon also offers a wide variety of classical concerts and occasional opera and ballet.

Lisbon's entertainment scene is as diverse as you would expect from a European capital city, especially when it comes to nightlife. There are bars and clubs galore but for the Portuguese – and for many tourists – the classic nighttime outing in Lisbon is still to a *casa de fado* in Alfama or Bairro Alto. A century ago, 'respectable' people were reluctant to be seen in a *fado* club; nowadays the danger is not to your reputation, only to your wallet as dinner shows and drinks are quite pricey.

Nightlife

When in Lisbon, do as the Lisboetas do and kickstart the evening with a glass of *ginjinha* (cherry liqueur) at one of the tiny bars around Rossio (see page 40). For an evening meal choose Alfama or Bairro Alto, with or without *fado*. Bairro Alto positively buzzes after dark with nightclubs, jazz venues and bars for all tastes, some opening their doors as late as 11pm, and clubs even later. The night is long in Lisbon – you can dance until dawn.

More mainstream are the dock areas west of centre where warehouses have been stylishly converted into fashion-able and relatively pricey late-night bars and restaurants. Doca do Alcântara and the more intimate Doca de Santo Amaro marina both have river-facing esplanades, popular by day as well as by night. A more central nightlife hub is Cais do Sodré, formerly a no-go area, now boasting cool late-night clubs, but still retaining vestiges of its red-light past. A relative new comer to the nightlife scene is Príncipe Real, with its trendy cocktail bars and cafés and thriving gay scene. The hip Intendente quarter, north-east of the centre, is another red light-quarter undergoing transformation.

Performing arts

Look out for flyers advertising concerts taking place in churches and palaces, some of them free of charge. The city's most important cultural institution is the **Gulbenkian Foundation** (see page 52) which maintains its own symphony orchestra and draws leading world orchestras and chamber groups. The **Museu Gulbenkian** (www.gulbenkian.pt) hosts recitals, classical music and dance programmes, including open-air concerts in its amphitheatre in

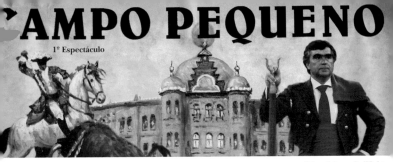

AMPO PEQUENO

1º Espectáculo

Advertising a bullfight

summer. Major symphonies and occasional opera are performed by the Portuguese Symphony Orchestra, based at the lovely rococo opera house, the **Teatro Nacional de São Carlo.** The Lisbon Metropolitan Orchestra performs countless concerts in the city and surrounds, including free concerts in Palacio Foz.

Most of Lisbon's stage plays are comedies and revues – in Portuguese. The best-known theatre is the **Teatro Nacional de Dona Maria II** on Rossio (www.teatro-dmaria.pt).

Cinemas tend to show foreign films in the original language with Portuguese subtitles. The renovated **São Jorge** picture house (www.cinemasaojorge.pt) on the Avenida da Liberdade has three screens and is a major venue for film festivals. Large shopping centres such as Amoreiras or El Corte Inglés have multiplex cinemas showing mainstream films.

Spectator sports

Lisbon is little different from other European cities in being mad about football. The city's two major teams are Benfica (www.slbenfica.pt) which plays at the Estádio da Luz and Sporting Clube de Portugal (www.sporting.pt) which holds matches at Estádio José Alvade.

Bullfights take place in the Campo Pequeno Praça de Touros bullring (www.campopequeno.com) from Easter to October. Unlike Spanish bullfights the bull is not killed – at least not in the bull-

ring – but as barbed darts are planted in its upper back, it remains a bloody spectacle. At the end the bull is led away among farm steers and is afterwards butchered.

Fado facts

Fado, the plaintive Portuguese song – literally 'fate' translated into music – is based on a story or poem and accompanied by the Portuguese 12-stringed *guitarra* or *viola* (acoustic Spanish guitar). Its roots can be traced back to the early 1820s and it has altered little since then. Lamentations of lost loves, lovers crossed or the forces of destiny are all characteristic themes. Guitarists start off the proceedings with a warm-up number. The lights dim, the audience goes quiet, and a spotlight picks out a woman in black who begins to wail out a song of tragedy and despair. Her sultry voice sums up that most Portuguese emotion, *saudade* – a swell of longing, regret and nostalgia. Sung by professionals, these chants are plangent, haunting and intensely moving, though to the unattuned ear they can sound strange and monotonous – hence the occasional jollification of traditional *fado* for the benefit of tourists. Most *fado* singers are women but you are also likely to hear a man perform the same sort of ballad with a strong, husky voice. In serious *fado* houses, audiences never interrupt the singer.

View of Lisbon and the River Tagus in the 16th century

HISTORY: KEY DATES

Fortunes have risen and fallen dramatically over the course of Lisbon's 3,000 year history. Its great days are over, but in recent years Lisbon has flourished once again as a cosmopolitan city.

FIRST SETTLERS

c1200 BC	The Phoenicians establish the trading post 'Alis Ubbo' ('Peaceful Harbour'), later changed to 'Olisipo', then to Lisbon.
205 BC	Romans create Lusitania; Olisipo is made a municipality.
60 BC	Julius Caesar makes Olisipo the western capital of Roman Empire.
AD 711	Moors from North Africa occupy Iberia.
1147	Afonso Henriques retakes Lisbon from the Moors and declares himself first King of Portugal.
1255	Capital of Portugal transferred from Coimbra to Lisbon.

GOLDEN AGE

1386	The Treaty of Windsor confirms England-Portugal Alliance, unbroken to this day. A year later King João I marries Philippa of Lancaster, daughter of John of Gaunt. Their third surviving son becomes 'Henry the Navigator'.
1415	Portuguese explorers reach Madeira, starting Age of Discoveries.
1425–1460	Period of exploration of the African coast by the Portuguese under Henry the Navigator; start of the slave trade.
1495–1521	King Manuel I on the throne; period of expansion and wealth.
1497–98	Vasco da Gama opens a sea route to India.
1500	Pedro Álvares Cabral lands in Brazil.
1543	Portuguese are the first Europeans to arrive in Japan.

SPANISH AND FRENCH RULE

1568	King Sebastião invades Morocco, is killed and defeated.
1580	Portugal falls under Spanish rule for 60 years.
1640	End of Spanish rule. King João IV begins the Braganza dynasty.

The 1755 Earthquake wrought terrible damage on the city

1755	The Great Earthquake devastates Lisbon – and other parts of Portugal. The Marquês de Pombal takes charge of reconstruction.
1807–11	Invasions by Napoleonic troops at the start of the Peninsular War; royal family flees to Brazil.
1821	The King returns from Brazil, handing rule back to the Braganzas under João VI.
1834	Prohibition of all religious orders and church property seized.

REPUBLIC TO DICTATORSHIP

1908	Popular revolution: assassination of King Carlos and Crown Prince in Lisbon.
1910	Republican uprising; the young King Manuel is deposed and given sanctuary by Britain, bringing to an end the Braganza dynasty.
1916	Germany declares war on Portugal.
1932	António de Oliveira Salazar becomes prime minister, really dictator.
1939–45	World War II. Portugal remains neutral on the outbreak of war.
1940	The Portuguese World Exhibition is held at Belém, emphasising the nation's independence.
1966	Opening of the Ponte de Salazar over the River Tejo, later renamed Ponte 25 de Abril to mark the Carnation Revolution date.
1970	Death of Salazar.
1974	The peaceful 'Carnation Revolution' restores democracy; Portugal pulls out of African colonies and a million expatriates return.

MODERN LISBON

1986	Portugal joins the EU. Redevelopment of Lisbon.
1988	Fire destroys most of Lisbon's Chiado quarter.
1994	Lisbon voted European City of Culture.
1998	Lisbon hosts Expo '98. Major building projects include the Ponte Vasco da Gama, Parque de Nações and the metro extension.
2002	The euro replaces the escudo as the national currency.
2004	Lisbon hosts the European Football Championship.
2007	EU leaders sign the Lisbon Treaty.
2011	Portuguese negotiate an economic bailout from the EU.
2014	End of the EU/IMF bailout programme.
2016	Portugal wins the UEFA European Championship for the first time.

BEST ROUTES

CASTELO AND ALFAMA

Soak up the city's history in Lisbon's oldest, most picturesque and beguiling quarter. Enjoy sweeping panoramic views, meander through the tangle of alleys in the Alfama and end the day listening to the strains of bittersweet fado.

DISTANCE: 4km (2.5 miles)
TIME: A full day
START: Castelo de São Jorge
END: Alfama
POINTS TO NOTE: Save your stamina for steps and steep streets later and take the free lifts or public transport up to the castle. A lift operates 9am–9pm from Rua dos Fanqueiros 170 in Baixa. Cross the square diagonally for a second lift which brings you up to the Costa do Castelo, a short walk from the castle. Alternatively take bus 737 from Praça da Figueira. Trams 12 and 28 go part of the way up to the castle but are usually packed with tourists. Pick up a plan when you buy your ticket for the castle – it can be tricky finding what's where. If visiting historic sites at the castle allow a couple of hours. Aim to be in Alfama in the late afternoon and early evening when the small tavernas start to open and stay late to enjoy the *fado*. Watch your valuables in the alleys of Alfama. The flea market at Campo de Santa Clara is held on Tuesday and Saturday, 8am–4.30pm.

The name Alfama has a Moorish origin, named after the hot springs once found in this quarter. But the neighbourhood is much older, dating from the time of the Romans and even earlier settlers who first occupied the hillside. A section of the Roman amphitheatre, buried in the 1755 earthquake and excavated in 1964, can be seen near the cathedral. Under the Arabs and in the early years under Christian rule, this was the grandest part of the city.

Earthquakes, and most notably the great one in 1755, destroyed most of the fine buildings and the quarter was eventually abandoned to fishermen and the transient population. What survives is the labyrinthine layout of the Moors, as well as a remarkable village-like atmosphere. The whole area on the slope between the castle and the River Tagus is a jumble of steps and cobbled alleys, with flapping laundry and hidden gardens and patios.

CASTELO DE SÃO JORGE

Crowning Lisbon's eastern hill is the imposing **Castelo de São Jorge** ❶ (St

Castelo de São Jorge crowns the hill of ochre rooftops

George's Castle, Mar–Oct 9am–9pm, last entry 8.30pm, Nov–Feb 9am–6pm, last entry 5.30pm; guided tours in English). The castle ramparts can be seen from many city viewpoints, serving as an apt and romantic reminder of the capital's ancient roots.

As you enter the ramparts you are stepping deep into the past. It was here that the foundations of Portugal were laid. In 1147 Portugal's first king, Afonso Henriques, launched a massive assault aided by rowdy crusaders, giant catapults and siege towers and conquered the castle, chasing the Moors from their citadel. The fall of Lisbon and the subsequent conquest of Moorish strongholds to the south ended five centuries of the Moors' civilising presence in Portugal. The castle became a home for the royalty and the old Moorish buildings were modified and enlarged. In the 16th century the royal family moved to the Royal Ribeira Palace on Terreiro do Paço (Praça do Comércio) and the castle became a military garrison.

Earthquakes and wear and tear over the centuries has left little intact but there are fine views, archaeological remains and peaceful gardens with peacocks strutting around as if they own the place.

WITHIN THE CITADEL

Almost every hill in this elevated part of town has a *miradouro*, but the best panorama of all belongs to the castle. From the shaded belvedere, where Afonso stands, statue in hand, all of Lisbon's history seems encapsulated: from the

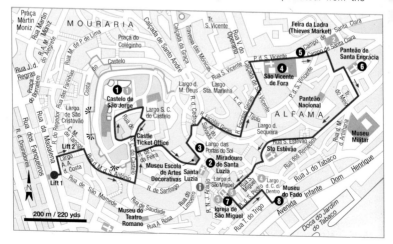

On the castle's ramparts

Moorish quarter of Alfama below, westwards across to the 17th-century warren of the Bairro Alto and between them the tidy grid of the 18th-century Baixa streets built to the command of the Marquês de Pombal. Following the river you can see as far as the 20th-century Ponte 25 de Abril, and beyond the bridge on a clear day, the Monument to the Discoveries and Belém Tower, launching point of the great Portuguese voyages of discovery.

After absorbing the views from the belvedere, follow the flow through the gardens to what remains of the original Moorish palace. The **Núcleo Museológico** displays archaeological finds from the castle, set out in glass cabinets under brick vaults. Exhibits span 25 centuries, going back to the Iron Age, and are accompanied by excellent labelling in English on a variety of themes, including Arab foods, currency and tobacco ('the saintly herb', thought to heal migraines, grout and other illnesses). If it's time for coffee take a break at the terraced café under the pines just beyond the museum.

Walk through the gardens and enter the castle via the so-called Tumbling Tower, today home to a **Camera Obscura** (daily 10am–5pm, subject to weather, guided tours every 15/20 minutes, in either Portuguese, Spanish or English) where real time images of the city viewed through a periscope are projected on to a screen. A guide pinpoints the main landmarks of Lisbon. Expect long queues in summer and no shows if it's dark and stormy.

Walk along the ramparts, climb up towers and, for the archaeological ruins, follow signs for the **Núcleo Arqueológico**. The site is divided into three parts: the 7th century BC, the old Islamic quarter and the royal residence. Unless you take a guided tour (free of charge) you may be not much the wiser, but it's a peaceful site under umbrella pines and there are lovely views across the Alfama.

Inside the walls of the castle, there is fine dining and fabulous views at the classy **Casa do Leão,** see ①. But for more affordable and characteristic Portuguese fare, have lunch later in the Alfama.

SANTA CRUZ QUARTER

Exiting the castle explore the atmospheric narrow alleys of the **Santa Cruz quarter**, by turning left along the Rua de Santa Cruz do Castelo, then right at the square, following the Rua do Recolhimento. You may well be tempted to take a break at one of the pretty cafés or little *tascas* serving seafood, and spilling out onto open-air patios. Back at the castle turn left, and follow the flow down to the **Largo do Contador Mor**, with its shady restaurants offering grilled sardines and sangria.

MIRADOURO DE SANTA LUZIA

Continue downhill, along the Travessa de Santa Luzia, for the romantic **Miradouro de Santa Luzia** ② This small bal-

Museu de Arts Decorativas

Around the castle walls

ustraded garden, with great swathes of bougainvillea and a vine-clad pergola, has stunning views over the sea of rooftops that cascade down to the Tagus. Two detailed and dramatic panels of *azulejos* on the church wall show Lisbon's waterfront as it was before the Great Earthquake, including the royal palace on the Terreiro do Paço. Told in tiles, too, is the story of Martim Moniz, close friend of Afonso Henriques: in the 1147 assault on São Jorge castle he is said to have seen the Moors closing the castle doors and sacrificed himself by holding open a castle gateway as Moors hacked him to death. The heroic act gave the Christian soldiers time to secure the gateway, and eventually capture the castle.

LARGO DAS PORTAS DO SOL

Just up the street is another magnificent *miradouro* at **Largo das Portas do Sol ❸**. The area is vibrant with life and colour as vintage trams and tuk-tuks rattle by and tourists throng on the belvedere to take snapshots of the Alfama spreading below. Presiding over the square is a statue of St Vincent, patron saint of Lisbon.

Across the road, the fine 17th century Azurara Palace has been filled with magnificent pieces of furniture, Chinese porcelain, a priceless silver collection and several tapestries from 16th to 19th century Portugal and its colonies, forming the **Museu de Artes Decorativas Portuguesas** (www.fress.pt; Museum of Portuguese Decorative Arts, Wed–Mon 10am–5pm). The museum belongs to the Ricardo do Espírito Santo Silva Foundation, which was established in the 1950s by the eponymous banker who bought the palace to house his valuable collection. The Foundation has 18 workshops where artisans practice traditional crafts such as wood-carving, metalwork, gilding and bookbinding.

SÃO VICENTE DE FORA

On the eastern heights beyond the dense quarters of the Alfama, and clearly visible from Largo Portas do Sol, are two remarkable churches. To reach the vast **Igreja e Mosteiro de São Vicente de Fora ❹** (Church and Monastery of St Vincent Beyond the Walls, Church daily 8am–1pm, 2.30–5pm, Monastery Tue–Sun 10am–6pm; church free, fee for monastery) either hop on a tram No 28 or follow the tram lines north, taking the right-hand fork down the hill to the narrowing and winding Rua das Escolas Gerais. Where the line starts to ascend and divides into two again, the church looms large to your right, its Mannerist facade ornamented with a variety of animated statues. *De fora*, meaning outside, reflects the fact that the church once stood outside the city walls. Founded by Afonso Henriques, after retaking the city from the Moors, the church was reconstructed in the late 16th century around the time of the Inquisition.

Looking to the Igreja e Mosteiro de São Vicente de Fora

MONASTERY

The entrance to the monastery is to the left as you come out of the church. Built over an enormous cistern, which you see near the entrance, many of the monastery's walls and its cloisters are sumptu-ously lined with decorative and patriotic *azulejos*. Between the two cloisters is the exuberantly decorated sacristy, below which, it is said, lie the tombs of the Teutonic knights who helped Afonso in the Lisbon conquest. On the upper floor, in the museum area, don't miss the glazed tiled panels of the much-loved **Fables of La Fontaine**, depicted in 38 tableaux. The former refectory serves as the Royal Pantheon of the Braganza family, the last dynasty to rule Portugal. Tombs of royalty include Catherine of Braganza, queen to Charles II of England, Carlos I and his heir Prince Luís Felipe, assassinated together in 1908, and Manuel II who went into exile in Twickenham, south-west London, where his mother had been born, when the Portuguese monarchy was overthrown in 1910.

CAMPO DE SANTA CLARA AND THE PANTEÃO NACIONAL

Take the alley to the left of the church for the **Campo de Santa Clara ⑤**. On Tuesday and Saturday all peace and tranquillity departs from the square with the colourful **Feira da Ladra** (Thieves' Market). It's worth browsing through the splendid selection of junk for the occasional gem. Fans of *funghi* should make note of the wonderful mushroom restaurant, **Santa Clara dos Cogumelos**, see ②, although it's only open for dinner apart from at weekends.

From the square, follow the brown signs for another pantheon, the vast

---

Santo António

On the night of 12 June, the eve of the festival of Santo António, the city pays homage to its revered native son with a cheerfully noisy parade down the Avenida da Liberade, followed by festivities in Alfama. Streets are strung with bunting, colourful lights sparkle in squares and alleys, sardines are grilled by the thousand, wine flows, music plays, people dance – and buy or sell pots of basil for luck. All are welcome. On the nights of São Joao, 23 June, and São Pedro, on the 28th, it's almost as festive. Just downhill from Lisbon's cathedral is the little **Igreja de Sant António**, built in 1812 to honour the saint. Known to the rest of the world as St Antony of Padua, to Lisboetas he is Santo António di Lisboa. The crypt, all that survived the 1755 earthquake, was built on the spot where the saint's house stood, according to local lore. St Anthony is invoked as the patron saint of lost things, and locals also appeal to him for help in finding a spouse; sometimes bridal bouquets are left at his altar in the cathedral, along with thanks for all his good work.

Flea market wares at the Feira da Ladra

Panteão de Santa Engrácia ❻ (Tue–Sun May–Sep 10am–6pm, Oct–Apr 10am–5pm), just downhill from the monastery. This grandiosely domed baroque building was begun in the 1682 but took nearly 300 years to complete, hence the Portuguese saying for a task never done: *'obras de Santa Engrácia'*. The church honours great figures in Portuguese history such as Vasco da Gama and Henry the Navigator; from more recent history are the real tombs of Presidents of the Republic and contributors to Portuguese culture, including the famous *fado* singer Amália Rodrigues (1920–99; which always has fresh flowers) and well-known footballers. A lift up (often with queues, but you can also climb up) affords a wonderful panorama of the city.

HEART OF THE ALFAMA

From the Pantheon square drop down into the picturesque heart of the Alfama by taking the Rua dos Remédios then fork right along Rua do Vigário for the **Igreja de Santo Estêvão**. Here you'll find yet another *miradouro*, with views of the river over tumbling rooftops and small gardens. Take the very narrow steep stairway, Beco do Carneiro, on the far side of the church, and cross the street for the narrow Rua São Miguel, with its little shops and tiny alleys and stairways leading off. (Or you can avoid the Beco and go via the airier Calçadinha de Santo Estêvão and Rua da Regueira.)

This brings you to the **Igreja de São Miguel** ❼ (usually closed) which dates back to the 12th century but, like so many of Lisbon's churches, was rebuilt after the Great Earthquake of 1755. The building just across the road from the church is undergoing renovation to become the **Museu Judaico** (Jewish Museum) in 2017; this was the Jewish community quarter in medieval times. If you're in the area in June, when Alfama celebrates the festas of the popular saints – for virtually the whole month – the neighbourhood is festooned with decorations and explodes with music (see box).

For a meal you could opt for the fashionable **Santo António de Alfama**, see ❸, opposite the church, or explore the

> ## Sé Patriarcal
>
> On the western fringes of the Alfama is Lisbon's 12th century **Sé** (Cathedral, daily 9am–7pm, free but charge for cloisters and treasury), founded on the site of a mosque. The church has been heavily restored but retains its solid Romanesque facade with twin castellated towers, softened by a rose window. The peaceful 13th century cloisters have been excavated to reveal signs of Iron Age, Roman and Moorish occupation all on this same site. The Treasury houses relics associated with patron saint, São Vicente. Legend has it that these were transported to Lisbon from Cape St Vincent in southern Portugal in a boat guarded by two sacred black ravens – the symbol of the city.

There is an incredible collection of vernacular tiles at Museu Nacional do Azulejo

Azulejos museum

Although out on a limb from the centre of Lisbon, it's well worth making the effort to see the unique collection of *azulejos* in the **Museu Nacional do Azulejo** (National Tile Museum; Rua da Madre de Deus 4; www.museudoazulejo.pt; Tue–Sun 10am–6pm; bus 794 from Praça do Comercio; free on first Sunday of month). The museum enjoys a magnificent setting in the Manueline Madre de Deus convent and is devoted entirely to this Portuguese art form. It was founded in 1509 by Queen Dona Leonor, widow of King João II. Rooms off the two-storey cloister show how the tiles were made and chart the development of the *azulejo*, from early Moorish origins in the 15th century through Spanish influence and the development of Portugal's own style. Thousands of tiles from over the centuries show gradual changes in colour and taste.

The interior of the 18th-century **Igreja da Madre de Deus** (Madre de Deus Church) is a heady mix of rococo gilt, frescoes, gorgeous *azulejos* and fine paintings. One of the museum's many treasures is the **Lisbon Panorama**, on the second floor in a room to itself. This fascinating view of the city is 23m (75ft) long, comprises 1,300 blue and white *azulejos* and records 14km (9 miles) of Lisbon's riverside as it looked 25 years before the 1755 earthquake. The tile theme continues in the attractive café, with 18th-century *azulejos* depicting poultry and game.

atmospheric alleyways and choose from cheap and characteristic eateries, with fresh sardines, paper table cloths and bills scribbled on scraps of paper. South of the church, turn left on to Alfama's main shopping street, the cobbled **Rua de São Pedro da Praça.** This used to be the site of a lively fish market with a cacophony of shouting fishmongers and families gathering together for meals in the street. Many moved out to quarters with better living conditions and nowadays immigrants and younger residents have replaced the fishing families. This is the main shopping street, with tiny old-fashioned groceries, family-run *tascas, casas de fado* and hole-in-the-wall bars offering one-euro shots of port or ginjinha liqueur. With the new generation and influx of tourism there is also a growing number of more modern shops and bars in newly restored buildings.

The Rua de São Pedro da Praça will bring you to the busy **Largo do Chafariz de Dentro**, named after the 17th-century fountain (*chafariz*), originally within (*dentro*) the city walls.

MUSEU DO FADO

At the southern gateway to the Alfama, within a revamped building which was Lisbon's waterworks' first pump house, is the **Museu do Fado ❶** (www.museudofado.pt; Fado Museum, Largo do Chafariz de Dentro, 1; Tue–Sun 10am–6pm). The museum sets the tone for the soul of the district, paying homage to

In the Museu do Fado

Lisbon's traditional form of song and its creators. Donations from the performers and their families enabled the opening of the museum in 1998. Pick up an audio guide (free with admission) to listen to bygone stars – or hear them in a mock *fado* tavern.

If inspired by *fado*, while away the early part of the evening in one of the local bars, then dine in one of the *casas de fado*. Just off Largo do Chafariz de Dentro is the well-known **Parreirinha de Alfama**, see ④, or near the Church of Sao Miguel is **A Baîuca**, see ⑤, a more low-key affair with amateur fado. A third option is **Clube de Fado** (Rua de São João da Praça 92, 8pm–2am) with well-known *fado* singers and no obligation to dine.

Food and drink

① CASA DO LEÃO

Castelo de São Jorge; tel: 218-880 154; daily 12.30–3pm, 8–10.30pm; €€€€

From the Pestana group who run Portugal's pousadas, this is the only restaurant within the castle grounds. Expect high prices, sublime views from the terrace and an elegant vaulted interior with a good range of international and Portuguese dishes.

② SANTA CLARA DOS COGUMELOS

Campo de Santa Clara 7; tel: 218-870 661; www.santaclaradoscogumelos.com; Tue–Fri 7.30–11pm, Sat–Sun 1–3.30pm, 7.30–11pm; €€

'The mushroom Temple' in Lisbon is how this Italian-run restaurant styles itself. Funghi features in *petiscos* (tapas), main courses and even desserts. Try organic shitake with coriander or mushroom ravioli with black trumpet sauce and end with porcini mushroom ice cream!

③ SANTO ANTÓNIO DE ALFAMA

Beco de São Miguel 7; 218-881 328; daily lunch and dinner; €€

Smarter than most Alfama restaurants, this has photos of films stars, a romantic vine-clad terrace and a 'no sardines or *fado*' slogan. It offers a good choice of tapas, grilled fish, traditional Portuguese dishes and salads.

④ PARREIRINHA DE ALFAMA

Beco do Espírito Santo 1; tel: 218-868 209; Tue–Sun 8pm–2am (show from 9.30pm); €€€€

Just off Largo do Chafariz de Dentro in Alfama, this one of Lisbon's oldest and most famous *fado* houses, popular with locals as well as tourists, though more for the music than its food.

⑤ A BAÎUCA

Rua de São Miguel, 20; tel: 218-867 284; Thu–Mon 8pm–midnight; €€

A characteristic *fado* venue in the heart of the Alfama opposite the Church of São Miguel. Dinner is compulsory, with minimum spend of €25.

BAIXA

Spend a leisurely couple of hours strolling through the heart of the city with its bustling streets and squares, alfresco cafés and old-world stores. From the waterfront the walk goes north to lively Rossio, ending at the Elevador de Santa Justa for fine views of the city.

DISTANCE: 2km (1.25 miles)
TIME: 2 hours plus, depending on visits
START: Praça do Comércio
END: Elevador de Santa Justa
POINTS TO NOTE: Route 3 could easily follow on from this route if you took the Elevador da Glória from Praça dos Restauradores at the end of the walk, rather than the Elevador de Santa Justa.

The Baixa has always been the commercial hub of the city, but before the Great Earthquake of 1755 it was a warren of alleys between the city's two main squares. The earthquake and ensuing tidal wave and fire left the area devastated, and it was from the ruins that the Marquês de Pombal, Chief Minister of King José I, rebuilt a new city on a grid street plan, with uniform, earthquake-proof buildings.

The fact that this was always a quarter of trade is reflected in the names of the streets: Rua dos Sapateiros for the shoemakers, Rua da Prata for the silver-smiths, Rua Áurea (also called Rua do Ouro) for the goldsmiths and Rua dos Fanqueiros for the haberdashers. A few of these crafts still exist.

PRAÇA DO COMÉRCIO

The Marquês de Pombal redesigned the monumental **Praça do Comércio ❶** (Commerce Square) as the centrepiece of his post-earthquake reconstruction. The square lies directly on the harbour, with marble steps leading down to the River Tagus. The Cais das Colunas, (Columns' Pier) was for centuries the main entrance to the city. Nowadays this is a popular spot for buskers or tourists who sit on the steps and enjoy the river views.

Lisboetas call the square by its old name, the Terreiro do Paço (Palace Square), after the Royal Ribeira Palace which was built here by Manuel I in 1510 but which was wiped out by the earthquake. The then-reigning monarch, José I, chose to move to the more stable parish of Ajuda, which later became part of Belém. An equestrian statue of the king takes centre stage

Praça do Comércio, Lisbon's impressive waterfront square

in the square, his horse trampling on snakes (symbols of evil) and the elephant representing Portugal's African and Indian colonies. A later monarch, King Carlos I and his heir, Luís Felipe, were shot in this square in 1908 as they were riding in an open landau with the king's wife and younger son, Manuel. Their assassins were shot on the spot. The first Portuguese regicide in centuries forced the young and unprepared Manuel to the throne. He would be Portugal's last king.

ARCO DA RUA AUGUSTA

Stately arcades and government buildings flank three sides of the vast square. On the north side the **Arco da Rua Augusta** ❷ (also known as the Arco da Vitória) is a triumphal arch crowned by a female allegory of Glory, holding laurel wreaths above Genius and Bravery. Heroic statues below (from left to right) represent Viriatus (the Lusitanian warrior who died resisting Roman expansion), Nuno Álvares Pereira (whose victory over Castilian forces ensured the nation's independence), Vasco da Gama and the Marquês de Pombal. The two recumbent figures represent the rivers Tagus and Douro. An elevator and steps take you up to the roof for views of the Baixa and the Tagus.

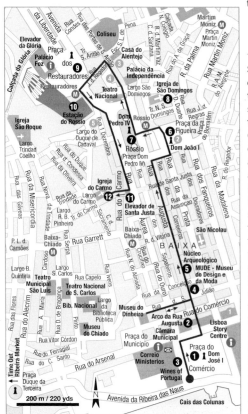

Ribeiras das Naus life

To absorb life on the square, choose one of the people-watching cafés, the most famous of which is the **Café Martinho da Arcada**, see ❶, east of the Arco da Rua Augusta. If it is after 11am you could sample regional wines at the **Wines of Portugal Tasting Rooms ❸** (www.winesofportugal.com;Tue–Sat 11am–7pm), located under the arches on the west side of the square. Purchase a chip card (minimum charge €3), take a glass and help yourself to 5cl shots from the taps. There is English labelling for each wine and friendly, helpful staff. With a day or more's notice you can also book a guided wine-tasting session (€6) and bone up on the diversity of wines from different Portuguese regions.

Across the square and within the tourist office building is the **Lisboa Story Centre** (www.lisboastorycentre.pt; daily 10am–8pm, last entry 7pm, audio guides in 9 languages), an underwhelming interactive centre which takes you through the major historical events from the foundation of the city to the modern day. The AskMe Lisboa office here provides free maps and abundant leaflets on the tourist attractions (there's also another office across the square).

The triumphal arch leads into pedestrianised Rua Augusta, the lively main thoroughfare leading north to Rossio. On the right is **MUDE** or the **Museo do Design e da Moda ❹** (www.mude.pt; closed for renovation), a striking collection of 20th century design and fashion, housed within a starkly converted bank building. The vault and second floor gallery are devoted to temporary exhibitions. The museum is due to reopen in 2017.

A short detour left along Rua de São Julião will bring you to the Largo de São Julião, site of the **Museo do Dinheiro** (Money Museum; www.museododinheiro.pt; Wed–Sat 10am–6pm; free), which opened in 2016. At a cost of 34 million euros, the Bank of Portugal has rebuilt the baroque Church

Riverside promenade

On the west side of the Praça do Comércio, the waterfront **Ribeiras das Naus** has been transformed into a pleasant, tree-lined promenade which has the feel of the seaside (there are even patches of sand). Open and spacious, it is popular with joggers, cyclists, strollers and sunbathers. The promenade leads to **Cais do Sodré**, a ferry terminal, station and former red light district which has been undergoing a major revamp. Apart from clubs, live music venues and bars, it is also home to the **Mercado da Ribeira**, the old domed market opposite the station which now has a wonderful food court, Time Out Market Lisbon, with gourmet kiosks open all day and evening (see page 117). Since opening in 2014, it has rapidly become the number one tourist attraction in the city – no mean feat in a city as packed with points of interest as Lisbon.

On Rua Augusta

of São Julião, previously used as the bank's vault. During excavations here in 2010 the 13th-century Wall of King Dinis was discovered in the crypt of the former church, and is now on display behind glass. The main museum traces the evolution of money in Portugal and around the world, with highly innovative and interactive displays. Visitors, for example, are invited to mint a coin or touch a 12kg (26lb) gold bar.

From Rua Augusta, take the next turning on the right, **Rua da Conceição**, a street traditionally known for its tiny haberdasheries. The lovely little Retrosaria Bijou at No 91 on your right is a fine example. Take the next left turn for the fascinating **Núcleo Arqueológico** ❺ (Rua dos Correeiros 21; tel: 211-131 004; free one hour guided tours in English or Portuguese, hourly Mon–Sat 10am–noon, 2–5pm), hidden below (and managed by) the HQ of Millennium BCP, Portugal's biggest privately-owned bank. An archaeological dig in the 1990s revealed layers of ruins, covering 2,500 years of history, and in particular the remains of a fish-processing centre which was located on the river in Roman times. Sauces and condiments were made from leftovers of fish, molluscs and oysters, soaked in salt and aromatic herbs. The mixture was heated in order to accelerate decomposition and then left to mature.

Continue along Rua dos Correeiros, where restaurants serving Portuguese fish dishes may well tempt you. The street is more old-fashioned and less touristy than Rua Augusta , though not without its restaurant touts. Turn left at Rua da Vitória (with views of the Elevador de Santa Justa at the end of the street, see below) and return to Rua Augusta for retail therapy and entertainment from frozen statues. At the top of the street turn right for **Praça da Figueira** ❻. Formerly the city's main marketplace, it is now a traffic-encircled square which could be bypassed were it not the location of one of the most famous patisseries in the city: the **Confeitaria Nacional**, see ❷, on your right as you enter the square. The equestrian statue of King João I, high on a pedestal in the centre of the square, was erected in 1971. With the king on your right, walk along the west side of the square, turning left for Rossio.

ROSSIO

The square popularly called **Rossio** ❼ is officially the Praça Dom Pedro IV, named after the king whose statue tops a pillar in the middle of the square. This is the true core of Lisbon, a large busy square and meeting place, with fountains and florists, shoe shiners and pavement cafés. The great open space was once the site of bullfights, carnivals, public executions, burning of Inquisition victims and other public events. The palace that served as the headquarters for the Inquisitor-General formerly took up the north end of the

Teatro Nacional Dona Maria II

square, but since the 1840s has been occupied by the **Teatro Nacional Dona Maria II** (www.teatro-dmario.pt; guided tours Mon 11.30am except Aug; tickets bookable online).

The two most famous cafés on the square are the **Pastelaria Suíça** on the eastern, sunnier side and the elegantly-fronted Art Nouveau **Café Nicola** on the opposite side, an ex haunt of artists, politicians and intellectuals. Both are good for watching the world go by, though you pay for the privilege and get pestered by peddlers.

If you spot locals or tourists gathering around tiny hole-in-the-wall bars in and around the Largo São Domingos, northwest of Rossio, they will be quaffing plastic shots of *ginjinha*, a sweet cherry liqueur which comes with or without the cherries (*com elas* or *sem elas*, with or without them). Two of the best known are A Ginjinha on the square (9am–10pm daily) and the nearby Ginjinha Sem Rival (7am to midnight) at Rua Das Portas de Santo Antão, 7 where Abílio Coelho has been making and serving the liqueur for 44 years. It's not to everyone's taste but it's cheap and worth a try.

Walking on art

Portugal is renowned for *azulejos* (see page 46) but another striking aspect of Portuguese identity is the *calçada portuguesa* or Portuguese paving. Everywhere you go in Lisbon you will see attractively decorated streets and squares. Tiny blocks of white limestone and black basalt are painstakingly cut and laid by hand to create patterns or images, similar to a mosaic. Many of the finest examples of these cobblestone designs can be seen along Avenida da Liberdade. The tradition was inspired by Roman mosaics, but today's patterned pavements in the city date to the mid-19th century, following completion of the wave design, known as the 'Largo Mar' (Wide Sea) in Rossio, honouring the Portuguese discoveries. You can still occasionally see pavers (*calceteiros*) repairing the streets, but the maintenance work is costly, the mosaics can be slippery and the number of craftsmen is dwindling. It may not be long before these fine mosaics are replaced with something more modern and practical.

IGREJA DE SÃO DOMINGOS

The burnt, cave-like interior of the Dominican **Igreja de São Domingos** ❽ (Largo de São Domingos, daily 7.30am–7pm) is an evocative reminder of the city's natural disasters: the earthquakes of 1531 and 1755, the fires following the latter earthquake, and another more recent fire in 1959. The walls and altar are charred, the pilasters blackened and battered. This is one of the city's most loved churches, with a steady stream of worshippers.

The cobbled and pedestrianised **Rua das Portas de Sant Antão** running north is flanked by restaurants

Estação do Rossio   *Elevador de Santa Justa's unique structure*

with touting waiters and more ginjinha bars. For affordable, filling fare try **Casa do Alentejo**, see ③, at No 58, or if you fancy some fine dining, the best bet is **Gambrinus**, see ④, at No 23–25. Inside you'll find a riot of interior styling: Moorish courtyards, Art Deco flourishes, a grand banquet hall and a restaurant decorated with panels of *azulejos*. If you just want to sample a few Alentejo specialities, there is an outlet next door with wines, cheeses and smoked sausage.

PRAÇA DOS RESTAURADORES

Across the road, take the Rua do Jardim do Regardor which brings you into the monumental **Praça dos Restauradores** ❾. The obelisk here celebrates the overthrow of Spanish rule in 1640. The square stretches to the broad, elegant Avenida da Liberdade, which runs for nearly a mile, and is famous for its smart designer shops (see Route 4). **Palacio Foz**, the pink palace on the west side of the square, houses a useful tourist office and hosts free concerts. Beside it, the lovely Art Deco ex-Teatro Eden is now the Eden Aparthotel, with tourist apartments and rooftop swimming pool. On the south side of the square is the 5-star Hotel Avenida Palace and beyond it the splendid mock-Manueline **Estação do Rossio** ❿ (Rossio Station) with horseshoe arches that make it look like a Moorish palace. From here frequent trains run to Sintra. There are fine views of the castle from the station

terrace, accessed via two sets of escalators. One of Lisbon's most popular restaurants, particularly with the Portuguese, is **Leão d'Ouro**, see ⑤, across the road from the station.

ELEVADOR DE SANTA JUSTA

Take the Rua Áurea south from Rossio, then turn right along the Rua de Santa Justa to see one of the most bizarre and intriguing structures in the city: the Neo-Gothic **Elevador de Santa Justa** ⓫ (daily Jun–Sep 7am–11pm, Oct–May 7am–10pm; Miradouro: daily 8.30am–8.30pm), a wrought iron lift built by Raul Mésnier, an apprentice of Gustave Eiffel. Be prepared for long queues, even off season. The lift is part of Lisbon's public transport system so you can use an all-day bus/metro ticket or a Viva Viagem card and go up and down at will. Alternatively you can walk up the steps – as the locals do.

The lift was inaugurated in 1901, the year electric trams began a transport service on the hilly, winding streets. The ascent in two wood-panelled cabins of the 45m (147 ft) high lift is brief but at the top you can climb up a spiral staircase to the *miradouro* (extra charge) with great views of the city.

A walkway links the lift to the lovely **Largo do Carmo** in Bairro Alto. End the day amid the Gothic ruins of the **Igreja do Carmo** ⓬ (Carmelite Church, see page 46), a moving reminder of the devastation wrought by the earthquake of 1755.

The ruins of Igreja do Carmo

Food and drink

① CAFÉ MARTINHO DA ARCADA
Praça do Comércio 3; tel: 218-879 259; closed Sun; €€

One of Lisbon's oldest cafés, dating from 1782, this is renowned as a former haunt of literati including the great Portuguese poet, Fernando Pessoa (1888–1935). Photographs of Pessoa and his favourite table have been preserved for posterity. Stop for coffee, ideally with a couple of *pastéis de nata* (custard tarts). Full meals also available. Pavement tables have views (and fumes) of trams rattling by.

② CONFEITARIA NACIONAL
Praça da Figueira 18B; tel: 213-243 000; Mon–Thu 8am–8pm, Fri–Sat 8am–9pm, Sun 9am–9pm; €

This is one of the oldest and best confectioners in town. It has been in the same family for six generations. The array of pastries is a feast for the eyes – as is the elegant, French style interior. The speciality is '*Bolo-Rei*' made to the original secret recipe, brought from France in 1850. Light lunches are also available.

③ CASA DO ALENTEJO
Rua das Portas de Santo Antão 58; tel: 213-405 140; www.casadoalentejo.com.pt; Mon–Sat noon–3pm, 7–11pm; €€

Once a palace belonging to the Viscounts of Alverca, since the 1920s the house has been the cultural and social centre of Alentejanos (residents of the Alentejo region) living in Lisbon. Its traditional restaurant serves excellent, well-priced and hearty Alentejo dishes for lunch and dinner. Typical dishes are *Açorda*, bread and garlic soup, lamb casserole, rabbit baked in the oven and regional desserts. Alternatively, opt for tapas in the simple *taberna* with a little courtyard.

④ GAMBRINUS
Rua das Portas de Santo Antão, 23; tel: 213-421 466; www.gabrinuslisboa.com; daily noon–1.30am; €€€€

One of the city's most famous restaurants, Gambrinus has a club-like atmosphere, top-notch traditional service and fabulous fresh fish as well as meat specialities such as partridge pie. The favourite dessert is Crêpes Suzette.

⑤ LEÃO D'OURO
Rua 1 de Dezembro 105; tel: 213-426 195; www.restauranteleaodouro.com.pt; daily lunch and dinner; €€€

Just off Rossio, this delightful restaurant dates from the 1840s and has vaulted ceilings, decorative *azulejos*, hanging hams and rows of wine. Seafood is the speciality. The tuna dip pre-starter is great value; then try the cataplana fish stew or the seafood rice with shrimp, lobster, mussels and prawns.

Elevador da Glória makes its way up the hill

BAIRRO ALTO AND CHIADO

Walk the warren of the Bairro Alto, shop in the chic Chiado,
then dine out, listen to fado or join the bar-hopping revellers.
The Bairro Alto boasts the coolest bars and clubs in the city.

DISTANCE: 3.5km (2 miles)
TIME: An afternoon, minimum two hours
START: Elevador da Glória
END: Bairro Alto
POINTS TO NOTE: Bairro Alto is served
by the metro Baixa-Chiado (blue and
green lines), Tram 28 and various
buses. Arrive in the afternoon, and stay
the evening to sample the excellent
restaurants and lively nightlife.
Advance reservations are essential for
Belcanto restaurant.

High above the Baixa, the maze-like
Bairro Alto (Upper Town) is a hilly and
dense quarter, full of picturesque peeling
houses lining cobbled, car-free streets.
Formerly run-down and sleazy, it is today
an area of family-run *tascas* (tiny restaurants), quirky, arty shops and bohemian
boutiques. But more than anywhere in
Lisbon, the Bairro Alto leads a double
life. Sleepy by day, it becomes the nightlife epicentre of Lisbon after dark. Very
different in feel is neighbouring Chiado,
long renowned for dispensing Lisbon's most elegant goods – silverware,
leather, fashions and books – along with
fine pastries and tea shops. It was once
a haunt of the literati, many of whom fre-
quented its famous A Brasiliera café.

MIRADOURO AND CONVENT OF SÃO PEDRO DE ALCÂNTARA

From Praça dos Restauradores, take the
Elevador da Glória ❶, the picturesque
yellow funicular which has plied the Rua
da Glória since circa 1900. (You may have
to queue – locals tend to walk up the hill
rather than wait). At the top on the right
admire the expansive views across Baixa
from the belvedere of the **Miradouro de
São Pedro de Alcântara ❷**. All the distinctive buildings are flagged on a large
pictorial tiled table. The view takes in a
great sweep of the Lisbon skyline from
the Sé (cathedral) and castle ramparts to
the 21st century skyscrapers in the north.

Just up the street on the left is the
**Convento de São Pedro de Alcântara
❸** (Rua Luísa Todi, 1, Apr–Sep Mon
2–7pm, Tue–Sun 10am–7pm, Oct–
Mar Mon 2–6pm, Tue–Sun 10am–6pm,

Rich detaila at Igreja de San Roque

free) which opened for visits in 2014. The highlights here are the glorious blue-and-white *azulejos* depicting *Scenes from the Life of St Peter of Alcântara* on the lower level of the church, the *trompe l'oeil* ceiling of the church and the funerary chapel of Cardinal Veríssimo de Lancastre with glorious inlaid marble.

SOLAR DO VINHO DO PORTO

One of the world's greatest selection of port wines can be seen at the **Solar do Vinho do Porto** (www.ivdp.pt; Mon–Fri 11am–midnight, Sat 3pm–midnight) in the 18th century Palace of São Pedro de Alcântara opposite the top of the Elevador da Glória. Managed by the Institute of Douro and Port Wines this is a prime spot to sample port. You can choose from around 150 (most sold by the glass), accompanied by optional cheese, almonds or chocolate. Tastings can include some of the rarer vintages and prices range from €2 to €25 a glass. Bone up on port from the menu, but don't expect a lesson from the staff. They are not renowned for cordiality, especially when the place is buzzing with tourists – which it often is.

IGREJA DI SAN ROQUE

Continue down the street for **Largo Trindade Coelho**, with its statue of a lottery seller and a kiosk selling the real thing. Overlooking the square is the Jesuit **Igreja di Sao Roque** ⑤ (Church of St Roch, Apr–Sep Mon 2–7pm, Tue–Sun 9am–7pm, Oct–Mar Mon 2–6pm, Tue–Sun 9am–6pm; free). The dull facade, rebuilt after the 1755 earthquake, belies a lavishly-decorated interior. The beautiful *trompe l'oeil* ceiling dates from 1589 and is the only surviving example

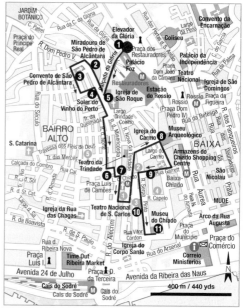

Painting at the Museu de São Roque

in Lisbon of a Mannerist style ceiling. Of the eight richly-decorated chapels, the most opulent is that of St John the Baptist, fourth on the left, incorporating lapis lazuli, agate, porphyry, alabaster, amethyst, jade and different marbles. King João V, Lisbon's most extravagant king, ordered the altar from Rome, where teams of artists and artisans worked on it for five years. The chapel was blessed by Pope Benedict X1V before being dismantled and carried in three ships to Lisbon where it was permanently installed in 1747. Either side of the chancel are two reliquary altars, containing relics of Holy Martyrs (men on the left side, women on the right), dating from the 16th century onwards.

Adjoining the church is the **Museu de São Roque** (Mon 2–7pm, Tue–Sun 10am–7pm) with a beautifully-presented collection of precious reliquaries, paintings, delicately-worked jewellery and 18th-century textiles.

STREETS AND SQUARES OF BAIRRO ALTO

Most of the Bairro Alto's restaurants and bars are in the narrow streets to the west of the Rua de São Pedro de Alcântara and this is the place to return later for a meal and a taste of the neighbourhood's nightlife. For a daylight impression of the narrow streets with their wrought-iron balconies and flapping laundry, take a walk from the square along the **Travessa da Queimada.** Explore the area with its grid of streets, then come south along the **Rua do Norte**, past the *fado* bars and down to **Praça Luís de Camões ⑥**. If you hear a bell ringing, make for **Manteigaria**, a patisserie just off the square at Rua do Loreto, 2 – there will be a fresh batch of their warm, mouthwatering *pastéis de nata* (custard tarts).

The Praça Luís de Camões is dominated by the imposing statue of the eponymous poet, with nine literary figures on pedestals below. Another literary idol lies close by in the Rua do Alecrim, beyond the square. A statue of the 19th century novelist, Eça de Queiróz (1845–1900), gazes upon a scantily-veiled muse in the Largo do Barão Quintela. Overlooking the square on Rua do Alecrim is the beautifully restored **Palacio Chiado**, see ❶, one of the city's new gastronomic venues.

Jardim Botânico

For a cool shady spot you may want to deviate north of the Miradouro, around 10 minutes' walk up the main Rua de São Pedro de Alcântara, for the **Jardim Botânico** (Botanical Garden, daily 9am–8pm, winter 9am–6pm, but closed for restoration until 2017). The walk takes you via the Principe Real quarter with lovely gardens, antique shops and hip stores. The Jardim Botânico is reached through the university gate alongside the Academy of Sciences. Founded in 1873, the tranquil lush gardens are rich in rare plants from distant climes.

Detail on the façade of Convento do Carmo

CHIADO

Retrace your steps, turning right at the top of the street for the **Largo do Chiado ❼**, overlooked by two Baroque churches. Turn left into the Rua Nova da Trindade with the Teatro da Trindade on the left. The theatre's heyday was the 1930s and 40s but it continues to host plays and opera. Turn right for the Largo Rafael Bordalo Pinheiro, with cafés, restaurants and, on the left, the 19th century **Casa do Ferreira das Tabuletas** with *trompe l'oeil azulejos* of allegorical figures representing Earth, Water, Commerce, Industry, Science and Agriculture. Continue down Rua da Trindade for the Largo do Carmo.

Azulejos

Azulejos, the hand-painted, glazed ceramic tiles omnipresent in Lisbon, are the Moors' most lasting legacy. Lining church walls, embellishing palaces and humble houses, gracing gardens and fonts, these ceramic tiles are a delight. The tiled panels are not merely decorative. Following the Great Earthquake in 1755, fires devastated much of Lisbon and the surrounding area and *azulejos* were widely used to protect buildings from going up in flames again. At the Museu Nacional do Azulejo (see page 34), which has a magnificent and comprehensive collection of Portuguese tiles, you can see how they are made.

IGREJO DO CARMO

The lovely **Largo do Carmo** with its tree-shaded cafés and fountain is overlooked by the former **Convento do Carmo**, HQ of the Paramilitary National Republican Guard where the prime minister and conservative leaders took refuge as crowds thronged outside during the 1974 Revolution. To the right of it is the entrance to the **Igreja do Carmo ❽** and **Museo Arqueológico del Carmo** (Mon–Sat May–Sep 10am–7pm, Oct–Apr 10am–6pm; in summer every Thu until 10pm).

On All Saints' Day in 1755, when the Great Earthquake struck (see page 11), the church roof fell on a full congregation. It has stood in ruins ever since, a mere shell but a highly evocative reminder of the catastrophic event. The roofless Gothic arches silhouetted against the intensely blue sky is one of Lisbon's most striking sights. The Carmelite church was founded in the 14th century and when it was built it was the largest church in Lisbon. The eclectic museum in the chancel has exhibits ranging from a Roman tomb, Spanish-Moorish *azulejos* and mummified remains from Peru.

RUA GARRETT

Take the narrow Calçada do Sacramento, which drops down from the Largo do Carmo into **Rua Garrett ❾**. In 1988 this fashionable shopping street

Casa do Ferreira exterior   *Rua Garrett shop*

of the Chiado was devastated by a fire which started in nearby Rua do Carmo. Many of the 18th century buildings were destroyed, along with shops and offices. The fire wiped out two of Europe's oldest department stores, including the legendary Amarzéns do Chiado. Portugal's internationally renowned architect, Álvaro Siza, oversaw the tasteful reconstruction of the neighbourhood, especially along the Rua do Carmo.

Turn left and you will find the rebuilt Armazéns do Chiado shopping centre, and just down the Rua do Carmo on the left, **Santini**, with irresistible ice creams. Head west along Rua Garrett, passing elegant Art Nouveau shop fronts, to **A Brasileira**, see ②, where Fernando Pessoa, Portugal's famous poet, sits at a pavement table. Another popular people-watching spot is **Pastelaria Bénard** next door at No 104, famed for its home-baked croissants.

RUA SERPA PINTO

From Largo do Chiado go south along Rua Serpa Pinto. You very soon come to a square overlooked by the **Teatro Nacional de São Carlos** ⑩, Lisbon's main opera house. This was styled on Milan's La Scala and has a lovely rococo interior, accessible during performances only. The **Café Lisboa**, see ①, within the theatre, is run by famous chef, José Avallez. Serious foodies who want to experience Jose Avallez's real culinary genius should cross the road

and, if not put off by the sky-high prices, book a table at **Belcanto**, see ④.

A two-minute walk down the street brings you to the **Museu Nacional de Arte Contemporânea do Chiado** or simply the **Museu do Chiado** ⑪ (www.museuartecontemporanea.pt; Tue–Sun 10am–6pm; free first Sun of the month). Stylishly redesigned after the 1988 fire, the museum exhibits mainly Portuguese art from Romanticism through to Modernism. The name is a little misleading, but there are temporary exhibitions with contemporary art on display. There is also a pleasant terrace café where jazz concerts take place in summer.

BAIRRO ALTO NIGHTLIFE

Head for the small bars and tascas in and around Rua Diario de Noticias late at night and you will probably be able to hear amateur fado – *fado vadio* – for the price of a cheap drink. Alternatively opt for *fado* and dinner. One of the best places is the long-established **O Faia**, see ⑤.

Café culture

Some say the custom of calling a small black coffee *uma bica* started at A Brasileira café. To promote its coffee, which many thought very bitter, the owners placed a placard outside which said *Beba Isto Com Açúcar* (Drink this with Sugar). The initials form the word BICA.

Bairro Alto nightlife is legendary

Food and drink

1 PALÁCIO CHIADO

Rua do Alecrim 70; tel: 210-101 184; www.palaciochiado.pt; Sun–Wed noon–midnight, Thur–Sat noon–2am; €–€€€

Enjoy gourmet offerings in the historic rooms of the Quintela Palace, amid frescoes, stained glass and stuccowork. Pick up an electronic card at the entrance and choose from different outlets: Portuguese tapas, *charcuterie*, gourmet burgers, sushi or maybe a platter of oysters with sea foam, passion fruit and seaweed, washed down with sparkling wine.

2 A BRASILEIRA

Rua Garrett 120; www.cafe-abrasileira.com; daily 8am–2am; €

Lisbon's most famous café opened in 1905 to sell Brazilian coffee, at that time virtually unknown in Portugal. Every customer who bought a kilo of ground coffee was given a free cup as they waited for their order. It was a favourite haunt among the literati, among them Fernando Pessoa who enjoyed a glass of absinthe and a sweet *bica* while he read or wrote or smoked. It was redesigned in art deco style, with a green and gold entrance and a fine interior in wood with mirrors, marble and stuccowork.

3 CAFÉ LISBOA

Teatro Nacional de São Carlos, Largo de São Carlos, 23; tel: 211-914 498; www.cafelisboa.pt; daily noon–midnight; €€

Savour some of Portugal's traditional dishes within Lisbon's opera house – or outside on the square where tables are shaded by white canopies. Beef croquettes, stuffed spider crab or octopus tartar can be followed by roasted codfish, partridge pie, or octopus risotto with coriander, ending with divine *pastéis de nata* (custard tarts). Meals, tapas, drinks or snacks are served at any time, and exotic cocktails too.

4 BELCANTO

Largo de São Carlos 10; tel: 213-420 607; www.belcanto.pt; Tue–Sat 12.30–3pm, 7–11pm; €€€€

This flagship restaurant of famous chef José Avillez received a second Michelin star in 2014 and Belcanto is regarded as the one of the best restaurants in Portugal, or indeed in the world. Revamped in 2016, the restaurant now has a larger kitchen and fewer tables. Reservations are essential.

5 O FAIA

Rua da Borroca 54-56; tel: 213-426 742; www.ofaia.com; Mon–Sat 8pm–2pm; €€€€

This iconic *fado* house, founded in 1947, still boasts big names. You can watch the show over a Portuguese dinner (served until 11pm) but note that the restaurant prices include the show and there is a minimum spend.

Looking back from the top of Parque Eduardo VII towards the Avenida

AVENIDA TO THE GULBENKIAN

A stately boulevard with top designer stores, tropical gardens within a park and a museum of world-class art are likely to entice you to this northern section of Lisbon.

DISTANCE: 4km (2.5 miles)
TIME: Half a day including visits
START: Praça dos Restauradores (Metro: Restauradores)
END: Gulbenkian Museum
POINTS TO NOTE: This is a good route to do on a Monday when the Calouste Gulbenkian Museum is open, unlike most of Lisbon's museums. It is free on Sunday from 2pm. Since the attractions are quite spread out you might want to use the metro. There are stops at Avenida, Marquês de Pombal, Parque and São Sebastião, all on the blue line. If you want to visit the Calouste Gulbenkian Museum without the longish walk through the park, take the metro from Marquês de Pombal to São Sebastião. Tables at Eleven need to be reserved in advance.

The route takes you up the Avenida da Liberdade, often referred to as Lisbon's Champs-Elysées, through the Parque Eduardo VII and up to the Calouste Gulbenkian Foundation. Of all the foreign visitors to Lisbon during the 20th century, Calouste Gulbenkian, the Armenian oil magnate, did more for the city than any other. He gave Lisbon the kind of patronage it needed and bequeathed his estate to Portugal on his death in 1955. The Foundation, supporting many cultural activities, is a rich and continuing part of Lisbon's fabric. The Calouste Gulbenkian Museum, housing his remarkable art collection, is Lisbon's top museum.

AVENIDA DA LIBERDADE

From Praça dos Restauradores the **Avenida da Liberdade** ❶ gently slopes uphill for a little over 1km (0.6 mile). This stately boulevard, simply known as the 'Avenida', was laid out in 1879–82 and is graced with statues, fountains, gardens and pavement cafés, shaded by palm and plane trees. Linking the old town to the new, it is home to upmarket hotels, luxury apartments, theatres and – at the upper end – the likes of Louis Vuitton,

Avenida da Liberdade has many upmarket hotels

Prada and Emporio Armani. At the top end of the Avenida is the huge traffic-girt **Praça Marquês de Pombal ❷** (or Rotunda) with the Marquês elevated on a lofty column with a lion by his side. He is gazing out over the city he rebuilt.

PARQUE EDOUARDO VII

Sloping upwards from the roundabout, the **Parque Eduardo VII ❸** is a park of well-manicured lawns, box hedges in geometrical design and mosaic-patterned walkways either side. The formally landscaped gardens were named in honour of Edward VII when he visited Portugal to reaffirm the Anglo-Portuguese alliance in 1903.

On the east side of the park, the **Pavilhão Carlos Lopes** – with tiled panels depicting scenes from Portuguese history – was originally built in Brazil for the Great International Exhibition of Rio de Janeiro in 1922. It was rebuilt in Lisbon in 1932, named the Palácio das Exposições (Palace of Expositions) and adapted

for sporting events. In 1984 the name was changed in honour of the Portuguese athlete Carlos Lopes. It is currently undergoing much-needed renovation and is due to reopen as an events venue in 2017.

In Estufa Fria   *The belvedere in Parque Eduardo VII*

ESTUFAS

In the northwest corner of the park is the **Estufa Fria** ❹ (Cold House, daily Apr–late Oct 9am–7pm, off-season 9am–5pm), a horticultural wonderland of exotic plants and flowers, bringing relief to the otherwise formal park. The Estufa is entirely covered by green wooden slats which keep out the sun but allow the air to circulate. It is humid without being uncomfortable, and absolutely still – not even the whisper of a breeze. Narrow paths weave their way through flowering shrubs, gigantic palms, exotic flowers and rare trees. Water is everywhere – ponds, small waterfalls, fountains and streams, plus cascades of water flowing down from rock-lined walls. At the far side, a doorway leads through to the cavernous **Estufa Quente** (Hot House), laid out in a similar way and visually just as delightful, but with its glass roof and walls you might find the hotter temperatures and humidity stifling in summer.

The park stretches up to a **belvedere**, with four soaring white columns and fine views over the city, castle and river. Cross the road to the Jardim Amália Rodrigues, named after the *fadista* (1920–99) known as the 'Rainha do Fado' or 'Queen of Fado' who helped popularise *fado* worldwide. If you want to treat yourself to something special for lunch (maybe the 6-course lobster menu?) try the restaurant **Eleven**, see ❶, or go for the cheaper option at the **Linha d'Água** café, see ❷, just to the east (beyond the little bridge) which has a lovely terrace by a lake.

From the gardens, take the cobbled path down to the main road where you will see **El Cortes Inglés** ❺, a 13-floor shopping centre (part of the Spanish chain) with an excellent supermarket, food hall and gourmet deli. With your back to the department store, walk along the main Avenida de Aguiar until you see a sign for the Fondação Calouste Gulbenkian, just before the major road junction. Walk through the park for the museum.

MUSEU GULBENKIAN

Around 6,000 items, from antiquity to the early 20th century, are housed in the **Museu Calouste Gulbenkian** ❻ (https://gulbenkian.pt/museu; Wed–Mon 10am–6pm, last entry 5.30pm; guided tours in English every Mon 10.30am–noon), created to house one of the finest private art collections in Europe. Calouste Gulbenkian (see box) amassed his works of art over a period of 40 years. Born in Istanbul in 1869, he had a passion for fine art and began collecting even before his deals in the oil industry gave him the nickname of 'Mr Five Percent'.

Surrounded by its own 17-acre park, the museum has spacious galleries with exquisitely-presented arte-

Sculpture in the Gulbenkian gardens

facts. Gulbenkian had very wide-ranging tastes. The **Coleção do Fundador** (Founder's Collection) begins chronologically with Egyptian ceramics and sculptures dating back to around 2700 BC, delicate and perfectly preserved. The handsome statue of the judge Bes is inscribed with hieroglyphs that date it from the reign of Pharaoh Psamtik I (7th century BC). A large section is devoted to art of the Islamic East and includes ancient fabrics, costumes and carpets, ceramics, glassware and illuminated pages from the Koran.

The survey of Western art begins in the 11th century with illuminated parchment manuscripts. Tiny ivory sculptures of religious scenes come from 14th century France and there are a number of well-preserved tapestries from Flemish and Italian workshops of the 16th century. Paintings by Dutch and Flemish masters include works by Rubens, Van der Weyden and Van Dyck, but pride of place goes to two Rembrandts, *Figure of an Old Man* and a painting of a helmeted warrior believed to be Pallas Athene or Alexander the Great, probably modelled on Rembrandt's son Titus. Don't miss the last room of the museum, devoted to the exquisite Art Nouveau glassware and jewellery designed by René Lalique. Gulbenkian admired it so much that he acquired 169 pieces when he was still young and not particularly rich – by his own standards, of course.

Calouste Gulbenkian

At the dawn of the Oil Age, a far-sighted Turkish-born Armenian put up money to help finance drilling in Mesopotamia, then part of the Turkish Empire. For his part, he received 5 percent of the Iraq Petroleum Company. Two world wars and the fuelling of millions of cars, planes and ships made Calouste Gulbenkian rich beyond imagination. He became a knowledgeable and dedicated collector of antiquities and great art, beginning with Turkish and Persian carpets, Armenian and Arabic manuscripts and Greek and Roman coins. His passions spread to include ancient Egyptian art, Chinese porcelain and Western painting. His mission was acquiring perfect examples in each of his chosen fields.

Gulbenkian, who held British nationality for much of his life, was preparing to travel to the US when he fell ill in Lisbon. He was so impressed with his treatment here that he decided to stay, establishing a philanthropic foundation to which he left most of his money and his entire art collection when he died in 1955.

COLEÇÃO MODERNA

A well-tended park with ponds, paths, sculpture and an outdoor auditorium connects the Museu Gulbenkian with the **Coleção Moderna** ❼ (The Modern Collection; https://gulbenkian.pt; Wed–Mon 10am–6pm; ticket covers

A Turner at the Gulbenkian   *The Gulbenkian is home to extensive artworks*

both Founder's and Modern Collections), forming part of the Gulbenkian Foundation. The museum is dedicated to modern art, from the end of the 19th century (where the Gulbenkian's collection concludes) to the present day. The works of art, which include installations and sculptures, are mainly Portuguese, though there are also some works by British artists. The collection continues to grow and is displayed on a rotating basis. The most famous painting is the portrait of the poet *Fernando Pessoa in the Café Irmãos Unidos* (1964) by José de Almada Negreiros. Much of the space is dedicated to temporary exhibitions of contemporary art. The museum has a popular café with an outdoor area overlooking the gardens.

If you've had enough culture for the day, wind down with a little retail therapy in the Corte Inglés shopping centre or if it's time for a spot of Portuguese cuisine try **De Castro Elias**, see ③, behind the museum.

Food and drink

① ELEVEN

Rua Marquês da Fronteira, Jardim Amália Rodrigues; tel: 213-862 211; www.restauranteleven.com; closed Sun; metro: Parque or São Sebastião; €€€€
Under German chef Joachim Koerper, Eleven (named after the 11 partners who set it up) acquired a Michelin star in 2006, only a year after it had opened. It's a rather dull concrete and glass block at the top of Eduardo VII Park, but has picture windows and panoramic views down to the city. Expect exquisite Mediterranean dishes, all using natural, fresh and seasonal products. Prices are not for the faint-hearted.

② LINHA D'ÁGUA

Rua Marquês de Fronteira, Jardim Amália Rodrigues; tel: 213-814 327; www.linhadeagua.pt; summer 10am–2am, winter 10am–8pm; €
Beside a lake at the top of Parque Edouardo VII, this cafeteira provides a peaceful retreat. Come for coffee, snacks and pastries any time of day, or at meal times choose from quiches, salads and a couple of fish and meat dishes, ending with a scoop of home-made ice cream.

③ DE CASTRO ELIAS

Avenida Elias Garcia 180; tel: 217-979 214; lunch and dinner daily; €€
This is an intimate little restaurant, with modern decor and a contemporary twist on traditional local fare. Try the tapas, shared plates or full meals, with dishes featuring *bacalhau* (salted cod), octopus, shrimps and other seafood. Adventurous carnivores can try *morcela* (blood sausage) with pineapple.

View from the top of Basílica da Estrela

SOUTH FROM ESTRELA

Wander through the well-to-do neighbourhoods of Estrela and Lapa, see a world-class museum of ancient art, then explore the cobbled backstreets of Madragoa. The lively riverside docas are an option for night owls.

> **DISTANCE:** 3.5km (2 miles)
> **TIME:** Half a day, with visits
> **START:** Basilica da Estrela
> **END:** Madragoa (or docas)
> **POINTS TO NOTE:** For Estrela take Bus 774 from Praça do Comércio, or Tram 25 or 28. The museums included are closed on a Monday.

To the west of central Lisbon, this quarter sees far fewer tourists than Alfama, Baixa or Bairro Alto. The route starts in the leafy Estrela district, then moves south to Lapa, an elegant residential neighbourhood with embassies and desirable residences overlooking the Tagus. The Museu Nacional de Arte Antiga provides a comprehensive view of Portuguese art from the 12th to the 19th centuries. The route also takes in the Madragoa neighbourhood, formerly a quarter of fishermen.

BASÍLICA DA ESTRELA

Set on a hill, the enormous domed **Basílica da Estrela ❶** (daily 7.30am–7.45pm, terrace 10am–6pm, until 6.40pm in summer; church free, but charge for the *Presépio* [nativity scene] and terrace) is one of Lisbon's great landmarks. The church was built in 1779–1790 at the behest of Queen Maria I to fulfil a vow she had made for the birth of a son. Sadly he died of smallpox two years before the completion of the church. Maria never got over his death and died insane in Brazil in 1816. She lies in grandeur in the right transept, in a particularly morbid affair of black marble, decorated with a writhing serpent, mourning angels and marble skulls. Tucked away in a small room is an enormous **nativity scene** carved by Machado de Castro, composed of over 500 cork and terracotta figures. A climb up 114 steps to the **terrace** is rewarded with extensive views over Lisbon.

Opposite the Basilica, the delightful **Jardim da Estrela ❷** (Estrela Gardens 7am–midnight, free) is very much a neighbourhood park, where children enjoy the duck ponds and playground and older residents pass the time of day chatting on shady benches. The

In Basílica da Estrela

tranquil gardens have lofty plane trees, subtropical plants, swathes of agapanthus and almost sufficient bird song to drown out traffic noise from surrounding streets.

CEMITÉRIO DOS INGLESES

Just north of the gardens lies the **Cemitério dos Ingleses ❸** (English Cemetery, Rua São Jorge, Mon–Fri 10am–1pm,

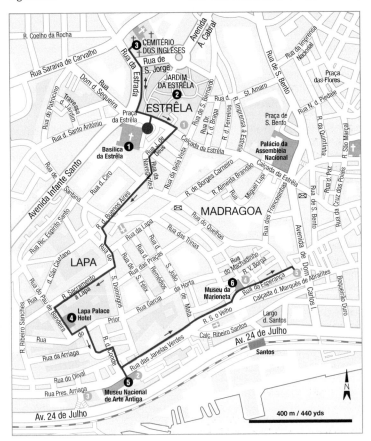

Headstones in Cemitério dos Ingleses

Sun 11am–1pm, donations welcomed). To get there, exit the gardens at Rua da Estrela, turning right and right again for the Rua São Jorge. The cemetery of the Anglican St George's Church, this is a leafy oasis with tree-shaded graves. A sign leads you to the raised tomb of the 18th-century novelist and playwright Henry Fielding, who came to Lisbon to improve his health, but died only two months later in 1754 at the age of 47. No one knows the spot where he was buried but a monument was erected to him in 1830. It is believed British soldiers were buried here during the Peninsular War, but there are no marked graves. The Commonwealth War Graves commemorate servicemen who died in the Lisbon area during World War II.

Return to Praça da Estrela, and for a coffee break try the famous 'convent' cakes and pastries at the **Casa dos Ovos Moles**, see ➊, on Calçada da Estrela, just beyond the pink convent, or at the Doce Estrela opposite.

Take the street going up (opposite the convent, with cafés on the left), then down Rua dos Navigantes and into Rua de Buenos Aires. Turn left into Rua São Domingos, then right along the tranquil **Rua do Sacramento à Lapa,** which is full of elegant embassies. A left turn at Rua do Pau al Bandiera will bring you to the **Lapa Palace Hotel ➍**, a lovely spot for a coffee or cocktail if you're feeling flush. At the junction turn left, then first right (Rua da São Francisco de Borja) and continue downhill for the square with the marble fountain.

MUSEU NACIONAL DE ARTE ANTIGA

Across the square is the **Museu Nacional de Arte Antiga ➎** (National Museum of Ancient Art; www.museudearteantiga.pt; Tue–Sun 10am–6pm), Portugal's largest museum, with several masterpieces of international renown. It is set on three floors of a handsomely-designed palace, though don't be surprised to find at least some of the rooms closed for lack of staff.

Level 1 is dedicated to textiles, furniture and paintings by foreign artists, including Tiepolo, Dürer (a self portrait and hypnotic *Saint Jerome*) and, most strikingly, the Spaniard Francisco de Zurbarán, whose six larger-than-life saints once belonged to the monastery of São Vicente de Fora (see page 31). The same floor also has a macabre triptych by Hieronymus Bosch. *The Temptation of St Anthony* (c.1500) is a fantastic hallucination, tempered with humour and executed with genius. A crane rigged up like a helicopter, flying fish taxis and horse-size rats fill this ghoulish nightmare.

Level 2 displays some exquisite pieces from the Orient, including ceramics, gold, silverware and jewellery, much of it from the Portuguese discoveries of the 15th and 16th centuries. Two finely-executed Japanese *Namban* screens depict the moment that the Portuguese set foot in southern Japan in 1543 – the first Europeans to do so.

The top floor is devoted to Portuguese art and sculpture. The highlight here is

Silver figurines on display *Polyptych of St Vincent*

the **Polyptych of St Vincent**, attributed to the 15th-century Portuguese master, Nuno Gonçalves, official painter to King Afonso V. It is a spectacular portrait of contemporary dignitaries, with masterful attention to detail of the individuals. Fifty-eight figures are gathered around St Vincent, among them Prince Henry the Navigator (to the left of St Vincent in the third panel from the left) in his large black hat and possibly Nuno Gonçalves himself up in the top left corner. Other figures are shown in every range of mood – ire, boredom and amusement – while several of the assembled clergymen appear as ugly, evil or both.

Revive yourself with liquid refreshment or lunch on the lovely terrace of the **museum café**, see ②, or at the modern **Le Chat**, see ③, just below the museum on the riverside.

Turn right out of the museum, along the Rua Janelas Verdes, then take the left fork by the large pink Igreja de Santos-o-Velho. Another left fork brings you into Rua da Esperanza.

MUSEU DA MARIONETA

Just up the hill is the **Museu da Marioneta** ❻ (Puppet Museum, Tue–Sun 10am–1pm, 2–6pm, last entry 12.30pm and 5.30pm; free on Sunday morning) with its collection of puppets in all shapes and sizes, beautifully displayed in rooms off the cloisters of the ex Convento das Bernardas. Crafted from gold leaf, papier mâché, wood, metal, leather, snail shell,

camel or buffalo hide, the puppets come from all over the world: Khon masks from Thailand, rod puppets from Java and Sicily, shadow puppets from China, Japan and Turkey, string puppets from Myanmar, and glove puppets from Italy and England. The oldest come from Asia and date back to the 16th century. Videos and touch screens show puppets in action (including Punch and Judy) and demonstrations of the painstaking creation of the models. The cloisters are the setting for the romantic restaurant **A Travessa**, see ④, open for dinner only. Book a table for later if it appeals.

Have a look at the streets behind the Rua da Esperança for a full flavour of the atmospheric Madragoa quarter, with its fading facades, flowerpots and tiny groceries and bars. From the museum take the first left along the Calçada do Castelo Picão and first right to explore the **Rua das Madres** and surrounding streets. At the end of the road turn right (Traversa do Pasteleiro) to rejoin the Rua de Esperança.

For a slap-up fish lunch or dinner continue along Rua de Esperança which joins the main Avenida Dom Carlos 1, then turn right for **Frade dos Mares**, see ⑤ at No 55.

RIVERSIDE NIGHTLIFE

For nightlife on the river, or an *aperitivo* with a view, head west to Alcântara, Lisbon's lively new neighbourhood. Buses and trams go along Avenida 24 de Julho

The Docas are a good choice for nightlife

but for two it's not much more expensive to hop in a taxi (you could also walk but it's not a very scenic route). The **Doca de Santo Amaro,** under the huge Ponte 25 de April suspension bridge, and the neighbouring, less intimate, **Doca de Alcântara**, where cruise-ship passengers come ashore, are collectively known as the 'docas'. Stylishly converted dockside warehouses have become creative hubs and venues for bars, cafés, clubs and restaurants. Relax by the river by day, dine or party at night (some clubs don't close until 6am at weekends!).

Food and drink

① CASA DOS OVOS MOLES

Calçada da Estrela, 142; tel: 919-303 788; www.casadosovosmolesemlisboa.pt; daily 10am–11pm; tram 28; €

Come to the 'House of the Soft Eggs' to try the famous egg pastries from Aveiro, along with the best of Portuguese 'convent sweets', made from ancient recipes which until the 19th century were religiously guarded by Dominican, Franciscan and Carmelite monks and nuns. The café occupies an old pharmacy.

② MUSEU NACIONAL DE ARTE ANTIGA RESTAURANT

Rua das Janelas Verdes; tel: 213-912 800; Tue–Sun 10am–5.30pm; €

This cafeteira has an irresistable garden terrace over the Tagus, dotted with statues and fountains. There is not a huge choice of main courses but what's on offer (pasta and at least one fish or meat dish) is wholesome and excellent value.

③ LE CHAT

Jardim 9 de Abril, 18-20; tel: 213-963 668; Mon–Sat 2.30pm–2am, Sun 12.30pm– midnight; €€

Just below the Museu Nacional de Arte Antiga, with a spacious terrace overlooking the river, this is an inviting spot for a drink. Meals are also available.

④ A TRAVESSA

Travessa do Convento das Bernardas 12; tel: 213-902 034; www.atravessa.com; Mon–Sat 7.30–midnight; €€€€

The candlelit restaurant has an alluring setting within a former 18th century convent, and tables are laid out in the cloisters on warm summer evenings. The menu features simply grilled fish or luxury specialities such as medallions of venison with black truffles.

⑤ FRADE DOS MARES

Avenida Dom Carlos 1, 55; tel: 213-909 418; www.fradedosmares.com; daily lunch and dinner; €€

This small, friendly restaurant has stylish modern decor and delicious fish dishes such as mussels au gratin, octopus cataplana with sweet potato or sea bass in filo pastry. Carnivores can tuck into steak, duck or pork; vegetarians into vegan risottos.

Torre de Belém

BELÉM

*No visit to Lisbon is complete without at least one day in Belém,
where exuberant masterpieces of the Manueline stand as symbols
of the Age of Discoveries. There is a wealth of museums too, and a
riverside setting, with inviting parks and gardens.*

DISTANCE: 7km (4.3 miles) by tram to
Belém; walking tour: 3km (2 miles)
TIME: A very full day, ideally two.
START: Praça da Figueira
END: Belém
POINTS TO NOTE: For transport to
Belém, alternatives to the recommended
Tram 15 are buses No 714 or 728,
or suburban train line from Cais do
Sodré. Don't go on Monday when most
monuments and museums are closed.
The Royal Palace is only open on
Saturdays. The main tourist attractions,
especially the monastery, can get very
busy in peak season and at weekends so
plan to visit them either earlier or later
in the day. You are unlikely to fit in all the
sights suggested in the route in a day.
Try and make an early start and if time is
pressing skip the monastery museums.
The monastery and Torre de Belém are
free on the first Sunday of the month.
Several combined tickets are available,
covering various Belém attractions. If you
are planning to eat at Feitora (see Food
and drink) reserve a table.

Belém, 6km (4 miles) west of the city
centre at the mouth of the River Tagus,
is a spacious suburb whose monuments,
museums, palaces and gardens make it
one of the most popular areas for visitors. Although the shore has changed
beyond recognition, it was from the river
at Belém that the great Portuguese dis-
coverers set out in the 15th and 16th
centuries. In 1487 Bartolomeu Dias
embarked on the voyage that would take
him round the Cape of Good Hope, opening the sea route to India, and it was also
from the Tejo shore that Vasco Da Gama
embarked on his journey in 1497, after
praying in a small chapel built by Henry
the Navigator. The chapel was levelled
shortly afterwards and in its place arose
the great Mosteiro dos Jerónimos. Along
with Belém's famous monuments are
an ever-increasing number of diverse
museums, the latest of which is state-of-
the-art MAAT (Museum of Art, Architecture and Technology).

Buses may be quicker to Belém but
more fun is the sleek modern Tram 15
(marked 15E, Algés) which departs from
Praça da Figueira, with 4–6 services an

Exhibits at Museu Nacional dos Coches

hour. It also stops at Praça do Comércio and Cais do Sodré but you are more likely to secure a seat by taking it from the departure point. You can buy a ticket on the bus or use a pre-paid Viva Viagem card which is cheaper. The journey follows the course of the Tagus and takes 25–40 minutes depending on traffic. Alight at the first Belém stop for the National Coach Museum.

MUSEU NACIONAL DOS COCHES

The former riding arena of Belém Palace, designed as a school for Lusitano horses, became the world's first coach museum under Queen Amélia (1865–1951), wife of King Carlos I. The **Museu Nacional dos Coches** ❶ (National Coach Museum; www.museudoscoches. pt; Tue–Sun 10am–6pm; combined

tickets are available with the Royal Riding School) is a unique collection of over 70 fine carriages, many drawn by royal horses on ceremonial occasions over four centuries, both in the city and across the country. The bulk of the collection was transferred from the palace on Rua Belém to a new stark white block across the road in 2015, so that the former arena, with its grand halls, painted ceiling and fine gallery, could be kept open as part of the royal palace, rather than as a museum. The coaches look somewhat out of place in the new functional venue but a few remain in situ in the Royal Riding School, which can still be visited.

Especially imposing are the huge carriages commissioned by King João V – one for his own use, and three for the Grand Legation to Pope Clement XI – with their extravagant groups of carved and

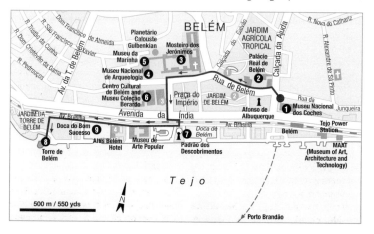

In the cloisters at Mosteiro dos Jerónimos

gilded baroque-style figures. The coach used by King José I, the berlin made for Queen Maria for the inauguration of the Basílica da Estrela, a charming 18th century French litter and the miniature carriage used by King Carlos I as a child are among the elegant exhibits.

PALÁCIO REAL DE BELÉM

After the coach museum you could cross the railway line to see contemporary exhibitions at the brand-new **MAAT** (see box) or cross the main Rua Belém where you can pop into the old coach museum in the Royal Riding School. Guards will be standing outside the main building of the **Palácio Real de Belém** ❷ (Belém Royal Palace, open Saturday only, guided 45-minute tours at 10.30am, 1.30pm, 2.30pm, 3.30pm and 4.30pm). A palace has stood here for five centuries, and from when it was purchased by João V in 1726 until the late 19th century it housed successive generations of kings and queens. The palace survived the earthquake of 1755, witnessed the departure of the royal family to Brazil in 1807 and saw the deaths of several princes. It is now the official residence of the President of Portugal. The Changing of the Guard, in which horses parade and bands play, is held in front of the palace on the third Sunday of the month. Saturday tours include the gardens as well as rooms in the palace.

Within the building, the **Museo da Presidência da República** (Museum of the President of the Republic; www.museu.presidencia.pt; Tue–Sun 10am–6pm) covers the history of the Portuguese Republic from the Revolution in 1910 to the present day – and sees more school groups than tourists. Unless you are heavily into modern Portuguese history, press on to try the most famous *pasteis de nata* (custard tarts) in Lisbon at **Pastéis de Belém**, see ❶. Sample a couple with coffee before continuing along the main street for the monastery.

MOSTEIRO DOS JERÓNIMOS

Thanks to wealth garnered from the spice trade and profit made from exploration, King Manuel was the richest king in Christendom. The most striking legacy of his remarkable reign, in which tiny Portugal dominated far oceans, is the **Mosteiro dos Jerónimos** ❸ (www.mosteirojeronimos.pt; Tue–Sun, May–Sep 10am–6.30pm, Oct–Apr 10am–5.30pm, last admission one hour before closing time; Church is free, fee for cloisters but free on first Sunday of the month, various combination tickets available, see website). King Manuel laid the cornerstone of the Hieronymite monastery in 1502, on the site of the chapel founded by Prince Henry the Navigator.

Interior

The monastery, declared a National Monument in 1907 and a World Heritage Site in 1983, is Lisbon's largest and most dazzling religious monument.

The Manueline style (see box) gives it its striking individuality. The convent wing was destroyed in the 1755 earthquake but the church and cloister survive. The south portal, facing you, is a brilliant example of the Manueline stonework, with intricately carved gables, pinnacles, saints – and possibly Henry the Navigator (though some historians disagree) on the central pedestal. Crowning the portal on a pedestal at the top is the Madonna, Santa Maria de Belém (Bethlehem).

The interior is lofty and harmonious with slender, ornately-decorated columns covered with vines and shoots, rising like palm trees to a graceful vaulted roof. The effect is one of immense height and space. Just inside the entrance, on the left, is the nautical-themed tomb of Vasco da Gama who died in Cochin, and opposite another tomb honours poet Luís de Camões, whose epic poem *Os Lusíadas (The Lusiads)* recounts the story of Portugal's early navigators and their discovery of the New World. The great poet was actually buried in a pauper's grave in 1580.

In the chancel are the tombs of King Manuel I, King João III and their queens (Manuel married three times; it is his second wife, mother of his 10 children, who lies here). Elephants, symbol of power and a tribute to the newly discovered marvels of the East, support the sarcophagi. In the south transept lies the empty tomb of King Sebastião I whose death in 1578 brought the Avis dynasty to an end. The young king never returned from battle in North Africa.

Cloister

Turn right out of the church, purchase a ticket for the cloister and join what is probably a long queue. It is well worth the wait. This is an exquisite and airy two-level structure of strikingly original proportions and perspectives. Exuberant sculptural detail decorates every arch, column, and even the walls. The adjoining refectory, lined with Rococo *azulejos*, makes a fine setting for occasional concerts. Upstairs there are good views down into the church and cloisters – as well as a bookshop and information on the history of the monastery.

If you only have a day to visit to Belém you may have to skip the monastery museums (Archaeology and Maritime) or, if you would rather concentrate on the old rather than the new, miss out on the Berardo Collection (see below). A lovely spot for lunch, when the time comes, is the **Rua Vieira Portuense**, with its row of colourful 16th and 17th century houses, and terraces overlooking the gardens and river. Take your pick of the restaurants, most of which serve reasonably priced, authentic Portuguese fare. **O Caniço**, see ❷, is a good bet.

MUSEU NACIONAL DE ARQUEOLOGIA

The monastery extends to the west, in more modern additions. The **Museu**

Mosteiro dos Jerónimos' striking white building

Nacional de Arqueologia ❹ (www. museuarqueologia.pt; Tue−Sun 10am− 6pm, last entry 5.30pm, some exhibitions may occasionally close noon−2pm) hosts temporary exhibitions along with a permanent collection, shown on a rotating basis, of finds from all over Portugal dating back to the Iron Age. The exquisite and beautifully laid out **Egyptian Antiquities** span 5,000 years from prehistory to the Coptic period (AD 395− 642), and the **Sala do Tesouro** (Room of Treasures) has stunning bronze and gold jewellery from the 3rd millenium BC, including many examples of torcs.

MUSEU DA MARINHA

Portugal's fascinating maritime heritage is documented at the **Museu da Marinha** ❺ (http://ccm.marinha.pt [Portuguese only]; Tue−Sun Apr−Sep 10am−6pm, Oct−Mar 10am−5pm) housed in the monastery and newer buildings around the Praça do Império. The journey follows the story of the Portuguese discoveries and their epic journeys to the East and the New World. A large statue of Henry the Navigator stands in the main entrance in what was once a chapel built by him where mariners took mass before their departure to the high seas. The oldest item in the museum is the delightful wooden figure of the Archangel St Raphael which accompanied Vasco da Gama to India and was brought back to Lisbon in 1600 by one of his great grandsons.

Exhibits include models of ships down the ages, navigational equipment, maritime paintings, charmingly painted ex-votos and replicas of 16th century maps showing the world as it was then known. From more recent times are the handsome royal suites from the *Amália*, the 1901 royal yacht named after Por-

Manueline architecture

The Portuguese may be principally known for *azulejo* designs and port wine, but equally important is the ornate style of architecture and stone carving that suddenly appeared in Portugal in the late 15th century. It flourished for only a few decades, mostly during the reign of Manuel I (1495−1521), hence the name Manueline. Probably triggered by the great ocean voyages of discovery, it took late Gothic as its base but added fanciful decoration and dramatic touches that were frequently references to the sea. Stone was carved like knotted rope and sculpted into imitation coral, seahorse, nets and waves, as well as non-nautical designs. The style first appeared in the small Igreja de Jesus in Setúbal (see page 93), then in the Torre de Belém and the monastery. It reached a peak of complexity in the unfinished chapels of the monastery at Batalha, between Lisbon and Coimbra. In the early 16th century the style fell out of favour, and by 1540 Portugal had joined the rest of Europe in building in the more sober Renaissance style.

The airy space at Centro Cultural de Belém

tugal's last queen. Pride of place goes to the huge galliot, or brigantine, built in 1785 to celebrate a royal marriage with seats for 80 oarsmen. The last time it was on the river Tagus was in 1957, carrying Queen Elizabeth II on a state visit. Next to it is the seaplane piloted by Portuguese aviators that made the first flight across the South Atlantic in 1922.

Educational attractions continue just to the west of the monastery with the **Calouste Gulbenkian Planetario** (Planetarium), which has shows at weekends.

MAAT

Lisbon's new cultural hub stands on the riverside in Belém alongside the 20th century Tejo Power Station. The brand new **MAAT** (Museum for Art, Architecture and Technology, Avenida de Brasília, Wed–Mon noon–8pm; www.maat.pt) is a striking contemporary building, resembling a gently-rising wave, which you can walk over, under and through. It was designed by Stirling Prize-winning British architect, Amanda Levete, and opened in 2016 as an exhibition centre for internationally renowned artists. The refurbished spaces at the Tejo Power Station (previously the Electricity Museum), connected by a garden, also host MAAT temporary exhibitions. This was the largest power plant in Portugal until the 1950s and the vast British-manufactured *caldeiras* (boilers) have been restored and are on view to the public.

MUSEU COLEÇÃO BERARDO

Due south of the Planetarium is the **Centro Cultural de Belém ⑥**. Built in 1992 this has a strong cultural programme and the **Museu Coleção Berardo** (Berardo Collection Museum; www.museu berardo.pt; daily 10am–7pm, last entry 6.30pm; free). One of the world's largest collections of modern and contemporary art, the museum displays the stunning collection of billionaire businessman and contemporary art collector, José Berardo. And all for free.

The collection presents a journey of art through the 20th century to the present day via its most significant movements and protaganists. Around 900 works of art are displayed on three floors, against gleaming white walls in a minimalist setting. The collection is set out with striking chronological clarity, starting with Picasso and the invention of cubism and ending with American Pop Art, featuring Andy Warhol's Brillo Boxes. The roll call of modern greats includes Salvador Dalí, Piet Mondrian, Joan Miró and Francis Bacon. Since it opened in 2007 this has become the most visited museum in Portugal and one of the 100 most visited in the world. The Cultural Centre has a choice of bars and restaurants including **Este Oeste**, see ①.

PADRÃO DOS DESCOBRIMENTOS

From the Centro Cultural take the subway to the **Padrão dos Descobrimentos ⑦**

Padrão dos Descobrimentos

The Torre de Belém is a hugely popular attraction

(Monument to the Discoveries; www.padraodosdescobrimentos.pt; daily Mar–Sep 10am–7pm, Oct–Feb 10am–6pm). Jutting from the riverbank like a caravel cresting a wave, it was built in 1960 to commemorate the 500th anniversary of Prince Henry the Navigator's death. Erected during the Salazar regime, the design has rarely been admired but there's a fascination about the stone figures facing the sea. On the prow stands Henry, looking out to sea; and behind him are the explorers, mariners, crusaders, astronomers, cartographers, chroniclers and others instrumental in Portugal's Age of Discovery. The leaflet which comes with the ticket shows you exactly who's who on the monument. Inside you can climb to the top for fine views of the city and river. From here you also have a good view of the vast map of the world at the foot of the monument, with key dates of discoveries.

TORRE DE BELÉM

Walk along the waterfront westwards as far as the **Torre de Belém** ❽ (Belém Tower, Tue–Sun May–Sep 10am–6.30pm, Oct–Apr 10am–5.30pm; www.torrebelem.pt), a Unesco World Heritage Site. This exquisite little fortress, erected to guard the entrance of the Tagus, is picturesquely set on the edge of the river, the site where Vasco da Gama and other navigators set forth on their explorations. Built between 1514 and 1520, it is a fine example of the Manue-

line style with its richly carved niches, corner turrets and shields bearing the Templar cross. Inside you can peer into a dungeon and climb the tower for fine river views, but its true charm is appreciated from the outside. It must have been a wonderful sight to weary explorers returning from their perilous journeys.

Towards evening enjoy a cocktail at a waterside bar, watch Belém glow in the setting sun and the light fade over the river. For dinner you could splash out on one of the smart restaurants at the **Doca do Bom Sucesso** ❾, the small marina east of the tower which is a popular night spot. **Feitora**, see ❹, at the Altis Belém Hotel has a Michelin star. Alternatively there are kiosks by the riverside for light bites or you could head back to one of the restaurants along Rua Veira Portuense for a simple seafood supper.

PALÁCIO NACIONAL DA AJUDA

In the unlikely event that you have a couple of hours to spare, or if you come back to Belém another day, consider a visit to the **Palácio Nacional da Ajuda** (www.palacioajuda.pt; Thu–Tue 10am–6pm, last entry 5.30pm), just over 1 km (0.6 mile) north of the Museu dos Coches. It's quite a hike on a hot day up the Calçada da Ajuda but a taxi from the square below will get you there in a couple of minutes. The palace is so colossal it takes your breath away. Work

The Marble Room of Palácio Nacional da Ajuda

began in 1802 to replace the temporary wooden palace erected here after the earthquake, but the royal family left soon afterwards for Brazil and the palace, which was planned to be double the size of the present one, was never completed. However under King Luis I's Italian bride, Maria Pia of Savoy, it saw lavish trappings including Gobelin tapestries, oriental ceramics, crystal chandeliers, rare Portuguese furniture, artworks and curiosities – all of which you can see today. Plans are in the pipeline to make alterations and have it as the repository for the crown jewels. Over the road is the **Jardim Botânico da Ajuda,** formal Italianate gardens, with 5,000 plant species from all over the world.

Food and drink

❶ PASTÉIS DE BELÉM

Rua de Belém 84-92; tel: 213-627 423; daily 8am–11pm; €

This is a long-standing institution, famous for its *pastéis de nata* (custard tarts). The relatively small shopfront belies a warren of rooms, all lined with blue-and-white *azulejos*. Here locals and visitors alike drink good coffee and enjoy the still-warm, delicate pieces of heaven, made to a secret recipe. You can also buy to take away, but be prepared to queue.

❷ O CANIÇO

Rua Vieira Portuense 30-32; tel: 213-630 593; lunch and dinner Tue–Sat; €

Join the locals on the terrace overlooking gardens in this simple family-run restaurant. The fish and seafood here are excellent value. Try the *pastéis de bacalhau* (salt cod fritters), the *açorda de gambas* (bread soup with prawns and coriander), fresh scabbard fish or skewers of octopus and prawns, served with salad and delicious potatoes in garlic and olive oil.

❸ ESTE OESTE

Centro Cultural de Belém, Praça do Império, Jardim das Oliveiras; tel: 215-904 358; daily 10am–11pm; €€

Within Belem's cultural centre, this café specialises in wood-oven pizzas and sushi, which is made in front of you in an open kitchen. The setting alone, overlooking the Tagus, is worth a visit – and you can come just for coffee or a drink as it's open all day.

❹ FEITORA

Altis Belém Hotel & Spa, Doca do Bom Successo; tel: 210-400 200; www.restaurantefeitoria.com; Mon–Sat for dinner 7.30–11pm; €€€€

Save this one for a special evening occasion. Chef João Rodrigues's cuisine is inspired by the spirit of the Portuguese explorers and his beautifully presented dishes combine traditional Portuguese flavours with Oriental influences. The restaurant is spacious and contemporary, with superb river views.

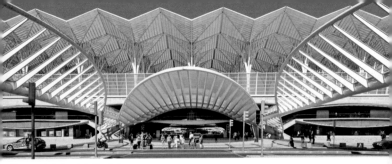

Estação do Oriente's bold exterior

PARQUE DAS NAÇÕES (PARK OF NATIONS)

This former wasteland was transformed for Expo '98 and couldn't be more different from the hilly city centre: a flat landscape with high-rise pavilions, a spacious waterfront – and one of the best aquariums in the world.

DISTANCE: 2.2km (1.4 miles; or more if you take in the Parque do Tejo)
TIME: Half a day
START: Oriente station
END: Parque do Tejo
POINTS TO NOTE: Arrive early for the Oceanarium (it opens at 8am) or book tickets online (www.oceanario.pt); it sees over a million visitors a year and the queues are particularly long on summer weekends. Set aside plenty of time for this attraction – many visitors spend half a day here. Take the metro red line from central Lisbon to Oriente station (around 20 minutes) or (much slower) bus 728 from Praça do Comércio. For refreshments the Oceanarium has a café and restaurant; the park has a choice of international restaurants with affordable prices; the Vasco da Gama shopping mall has cafés and snack bars, or a supermarket for a picnic.

You might just see the park as an international concrete strip, with no heart or soul, and rather fading at the edges. Or you might view it as a great day out with the kids: a stunning oceanarium (voted the best aquarium in the world on Trip Advisor), a science museum with great activities, pedestrianised walkways, cycle paths and cable cars which rise above the park and river. It's also popular with aficionados of contemporary architecture thanks to its stunning Oriente station and striking pavilions along the waterfront.

EXPO LEGACY

Prior to Lisbon's Expo '98, the eastern end of the Lisbon waterfront was an ugly and mainly derelict industrial site. Held on the 500th anniversary of Vasco da Gama's epic voyage to India, Expo provided an opportunity to revitalise the area, employing some of the world's most innovative architects to create a high-tech entertainment park/leisure zone. The theme was *The Oceans, a Heritage for the Future.* Framing the park is the futuristic railway station, a pristine shopping mall and the sleek white Ponte Vasco da Gama (Vasco da Gama Bridge), extending across the Tagus into the horizon.

The metro surfaces at the mainline station, **Estação do Oriente ❶**, with a stunning top level glass roof. This is Portugal's busiest station (combining bus, train and metro), designed by Spanish architect Santiago Calatrava as a major terminal for destinations around the country. Alighting from the metro, walk through the glass-roofed, 3-tiered **Centro Vasco da Gama ❷** shopping mall (daily 9am–midnight, www.centrovasco dagama.pt) with good views from the top. Also designed by Calatrava, it has the feel of a cruise ship, and has viewing terraces back and front.

The Parque das Nações complex extends 5km (3 miles) along the riverfront. The estuary is so wide here it feels like the sea. Keep-fit enthusiasts jog along the waterfront and fishermen cast their lines into the Tagus, but most tourists head straight for the oceanarium.

OCEANÁRIO

Go south along the Alameda dos Oceanos for the **Oceanário di Lisboa ❸** (Oceanarium; www.oceanario.pt; daily 10am–8pm, last entry 7pm, Nov–Mar 10am–6pm, last entry 5pm), the park's major attraction. Designed by American architect Peter Chermayeff and surrounded by water, the structure resembles a marooned oil derrick or space station from the set of a sci-fi thriller. Reached by a footbridge, it houses large tanks representing four distinct marine ecosystems: Antarctic, Indian, Pacific and Atlantic, but creating the illusion of a single aquarium and a sole ocean.

There are over 8,000 examples of sea creatures in 7 million litres of saltwater. You'll see Magellanic and crested rockhopper penguins in the Antarctic section

Oceanário di Lisboa is a world-class aquarium

and sea otters in the Pacific. As visitors make their way around the massive circular aquarium, tiger sharks, manta rays and schools of brightly coloured exotic fish glide silently by, overhead and beneath the observation decks. It is one of the few aquariums in the world to house the Ocean sunfish.

Children love it, but adults are usually hooked too. Visit the website for activities from guided tours to a sleepover with sharks!

PAVILHÃO DO CONHECIMENTO

On the Alameda dos Oceanos, just inland and south from the Oceanarium, the **Pavilhão do Conhecimento** ❹ (Pavilion of Knowledge; www.pavconhecimento.pt; Tue–Fri 10am–6pm, Sat–Sun 11am–7pm) is a highly-educational interactive museum of science and technology with some fascinating exhibitions and thrilling experiments for all ages. Beyond the museum, the **Jardins da Água** (Water Gardens) has water jets, waterfalls and benches under palm trees and provides a cool retreat in mid-summer.

THE WATERFRONT

For a bird's eye view over the river and park, you can take the **Telecabine** ❺ (Cable car; www.telecabinelisboa.pt; daily June–mid-Sep 10.30am–8pm, mid-Sep–late Oct, Mar and Apr 11am–7pm, late Oct–Feb 11am–6pm) which runs from the Oceanarium for about a kilo-

metre (0.6 mile) over the Olivais Docks to the Vasco da Gama tower – with the option of a return trip. Alternatively it's a very pleasant walk along the riverside promenade, on the east side of the Doca dos Oliviais. This runs all the way to the Vasco da Gama Bridge.

Overlooking the **Olivais Dock** is the prize-winning **Pavilhão de Portugal** ❻, a multipurpose arena designed by leading Portuguese architect Álvaro Siza Vieira. The pavilion has an astonishing curved concrete roof, suspended over its forecourt. Beyond it you'll see one of the many notable artworks in the park: Antony Gormley's iron statue *Rhizone*, representing nine figures. North of the marina is the space-ship-like **MEO Arena** ❼ (formerly the Pavilhão Atlântico) which hosts public events of up to 20,000 spectators and is Portugal's largest indoor arena and venue for sporting events.

You'll find a variety of options for lunch along the **Rua da Pimenta**, bordered by terraces with views of the **Jardim Garcia da Orta** ❽ and the river beyond. **Senhor Peixe**, see ❶, and **D'Bacalhau**, see ❷, are the best bets for fish. Another option is a picnic in the **Parque do Tejo** (Tagus Park) a large green area with bike trails and walks by the river extending beyond the 150m (492ft)-high **Torre Vasco da Gama** ❾ (Vasco da Gama Tower). Formerly part of an oil refinery, the tower was fashioned to look like a caravel. It is now integrated into the luxury **Myriad by Sana hotel**, whose restaurant, see ❸, has fine views of the estuary.

Ponte Vasco da Gama at sunrise

PONTE VASCO DA GAMA

The massive 17.2km (10.75 miles) **Ponte Vasco da Gama** spans the shallow but wide Tagus Estuary, stretching out seamlessly into the horizon. Including viaducts, it is the longest bridge in Europe.

A second bridge across the River Tagus had become essential to alleviate the congestion on the Ponte 25 de Abril. To finance it, the Portuguese government contracted the building to a private consortium, Lusoponte, who hold exclusive control of toll collection of both Lisbon's bridges for 40 years.

The bridge was designed to withstand earthquakes 4.5 times stronger than the historic Lisbon earthquake of 1755. The engineering marvel was completed in three years, and opened just in time for Expo '98. Before the opening it set a Guinness world record for amassing 15,000 Portuguese to feast on the largest *feijoada* (bean stew) ever, served at a 3 mile (5km) long table along the deck.

Food and drink

🔴 SENHOR PEIXE

Rua da Pimenta 35; tel: 218-955 892; www.senhorpeixe.pt; closed Mon and dinner Sun; €€

The lobsters in the tank and wonderful array of fish inside are likely to lure you into Senhor Peixe (Mr Fish). Usually buzzing with Portuguese, the restaurant offers around 20 different types of fish, mostly priced by the kilo. Among the specialities are *arroz de lagosta* (lobster risotto), *choco frito* (fried cuttle fish) and a wonderful *caldeirada* (fish stew) for two. Reserve a table on the terrace for river views across the gardens.

🔵 RESTAURANTE D'BACALHAU

Rua Pimenta 45; tel: 281-941 296; www.restaurantebacalhau.com; daily noon–4pm, 7–11pm; €€

Bacalhau (salted cod) is king at this restaurant, steps away from the Tagus. It is served in around ten different ways, from *lagueirada de bacalhau* with egg, spinach and chickpeas to the popular *com natas*, baked in cream sauce with potatoes. You can try a selection of four by opting for *mezcla de bacalhau* (codfish mix, for a minimum of two). Other options are a skewer of grouper, braised salmon or grilled octopus.

🔵 MYRIAD BY SANA HOTEL

Cais das Naus, Lote 2.21.01; tel: 211-107 600; www.myriad.pt; daily lunch and dinner; buffet weekdays 12.30–3.30pm, brunch weekends noon–4pm; €€€

If you want to be right on the river, head for the lounge restaurant of the Myriad by Sana hotel, located on the Tagus with fine views of the Vasco da Gama bridge. It serves an excellent light buffet, with optional chef's specials, or offers *à la carte*. The setting is contemporary, the service professional.

The view from Cristo Rei

CRISTO REI

Set on the south bank of the Tagus, the Cristo Rei monument is so big you're bound to spy it at some stage during your visit to Lisbon; but it's fun to take the ferry across for a sensational panorama from the 82 metre (269ft)-high viewing platform.

DISTANCE: Ferry (return trip) 6km (4 miles), Bus (return trip) 7km (4.4 miles)

TIME: A half day

START: Cais do Sodré

END: Cacilhas

POINTS TO NOTE: Choose a clear bright day. Ferries depart from Cais do Sodré at least four times an hour. Try to avoid weekends and returning during rush hour (5–7.30pm). There are often queues for the lift up the Cristo Rei but even at ground level the views are spectacular. If you visit the Cristo Rei in the morning you could always take a bus from Cacilhas to the Costa da Caparica (approx 35 minutes), home to some of the most pleasant beaches in the Lisbon area.

Lisboetas call it Outra Banda, the other shore, meaning the other bank of the River Tejo, long neglected because of the inconvenience of getting there. This changed after 1966 with the completion of what was then Europe's long-est suspension bridge, the Ponte 25 de Abril, and changed yet again with the opening of the rail link in 1999. A second bridge, the Vasco da Gama, opened in 1998 to relieve the ever-growing pressure on the first bridge.

Echoing the iconic Christ the Redeemer statue in Rio de Janeiro, the

Cristo Rei is visible from afar

Cristo Rei stands high above Lisbon across the river, just west of the Ponte 25 de Abril. The monument was built in 1949–1959 under the Salazar dictatorship as a sign of gratitude to God for saving Portugal from involvement in World War II.

HOW TO GET THERE

At **Cais do Sodré** ❶ follow signs for the *Terminal Fluvial* (Ferry Terminal). Buy a return ticket to **Cacilhas** ❷, hop on one of the orange ferries and enjoy the 15-minute ride. Cacilhas itself is nothing to write home about but it is a popular weekend and evening destination for Lisboetas for its seafood restaurants. *Caldeirada a fragateira*, a tasty fish stew, is a speciality, as are piles of fresh sardines, often cooked on smoking grills outdoors.

From Cacilhas you can take a taxi or the No 101 Cristo Rei bus, which departs regularly for the Cristo Rei monument, where it terminates. When you

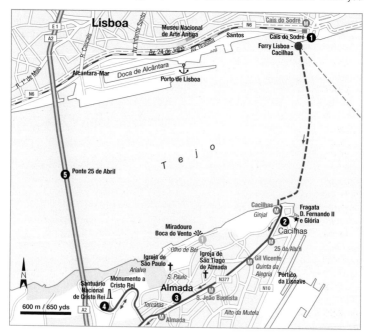

Ponte 25 de Abril with Cristo Rei on the left

arrive at the ferry dock, turn left for Platform 20 where the bus departs. The journey time is around 15 minutes. Tickets can be bought on board.

SANTUÁRIO NACIONAL DE CRISTO REI

The bus goes through the town of **Almada** ❸ and up to the **Santuário Nacional de Cristo Rei** ❹ (National Sanctuary of Christ the King; www.cristorei.pt; Mon–Fri 9.30am–6.30pm, Sat–Sun until 7pm, winter daily 9.30am–6.15pm; charge for lift). The visitors here are a mix of Portuguese pilgrims paying their respects in the chapel of the Catholic Welcome Centre and tourists taking arms-outstretched selfies. Mass is held here every Sunday.

The tall, solitary statue stands proud at 110m (360ft), of which 82m (269ft) are pedestal and 28m (91ft) the robed figure, blessing the city. Views from west to east embrace Belém, the Ponte 25 de Abril, downtown Lisbon, Castelo de São Jorge and the second bridge, the Ponte Vasco da Gama. On a clear day you can see as far as the Sierra of Sintra with the Palace of Pena on the hilltop. There may be a huge queue for the elevator but even at ground level there are spectacular views.

PONTE 25 DE ABRIL

The **Ponte 25 de Abril** ❺, which the statue overlooks, was also built under Portugal's long-time dictator, Salazar. Inspired by San Francisco's Golden Gate Bridge, it was originally called the Ponte Salazar but was renamed in honour of the bloodless revolution of 25 April 1974 which restored democracy to Portugal. In 1999 the lower tier of the bridge was adapted to accommodate a railway across the river. An 80m-high glass viewing platform is planned for the bridge in 2019.

For refreshment there is a café at the base of the monument, or for a good seafood lunch or dinner, head for **Atira-Te ao rio**, see ❶, at Cais do Ginjal, about 1km (half a mile) west of the Cacilhas ferry stop.

Food and drink

❶ ATIRA-TE AO RIO

Cais do Gingal, 69/70, Almada; tel: 212-751 380; www.atirateaorio.pt; closed Sun and Wed evening; €€

Enjoy stunning views of the city's skyline from the water's edge, while tucking into seafood from the simple menu. Shrimp soup or salad can be followed by a delicious *caldeirada de peixes e mariscos* (fish and seafood stew for two), or a Portuguese favourite: *bacalhau a lagareiro* (salted codfish in garlicky virgin olive oil, with little roasted potatoes, cooked in their skin). If you are here in the early evening, come in time to watch the sun sink behind the Ponte 25 de Abril.

One of Lisbon's iconic yellow trams

TRAM 28

Don't leave Lisbon without a trip on the city's vintage Tram No 28.
Oozing tradition and charm, this little yellow gem rattles and lurches
its way through the city's most picturesque and historic quarters.

DISTANCE: 7km (4.3 miles)
TIME: Approx 50 minutes (or longer depending on traffic)
START: Praça Martim Moniz, northeast of Rossio; metro: Martim Moniz, green line
END: Estrela or Campo de Ourique (Prazeres)
POINTS TO NOTE: This is the most popular route in Lisbon and trams are usually packed with tourists. You can pick up the No. 28 in the Alfama, at the Sé (cathedral) or on Rua da Conceição in the Baixa but for the best chance of securing a seat, get on at the starting point at Praça Martim Moniz. You can buy a ticket on the bus, though it works out cheaper if you use the rechargeable Via Viagem pre-paid ticket (see page 124), or you can use a Carris/metro pass. Trams run from 5.40am to around 9pm and depart roughly every 10 minutes, less frequently early am or late pm. Stops are indicated by large signs marked *paragem* (stop). The tram is a favourite of pickpockets so keep a careful eye on valuables.

Lisbon has five tram lines. Those servicing Baixa and Belém are modernised and have sleek interiors but the rest are pre-war. The system of electric tramways (*eléctricos*) started in 1901 and has been going strong ever since. These vintage trams, with their brightly painted yellow exteriors and wood-panelled interiors, are a great way of seeing the city. The most famous and picturesque is No 28, which offers an excellent sightseeing tour of old Lisbon.

Don't take this route if you are in a hurry. Just enjoy the ride and the opportunity to peer into tiny dark shop doorways, admire the geraniums on the balconies and the occasional glimpse of the river over the rooftops. Delays and crowds can mean a wait for a tram or one that you can get on, so this experience is one for a relaxed day.

As an alternative, Tram 12 has a limited service, but tends to be slightly less crowded. It departs from Praça da Figueira, doing a picturesque loop around the castle and the Alfama.

Tourists and locals alike crowd the trams so get on early

SETTING OFF

Catch Tram 28 at **Praça Martim Moniz ❶**, ideally no later than 8am if you want to secure a seat. Grab a window seat if you can, preferably on the left hand side which will give you the best views. Although you may be tempted to hop off the tram mid-way, you would be lucky to get a seat on another No 28 (and that's not just in high season). To guarantee a seat all the way, it's best to play it safe and stay put.

The tram will be marked Prazeres and it heads north along the Avenida Almirante de Reis, passing through Indendente, a former no-go area, now undergoing a dramatic revamp with an increasing number of hip shops and stylish cafés.

GRAÇA AND ALFAMA

The tram heads up to the charming **Graça ❷** neighbourhood, located on the hill above the imposing church and monastery of São Vicente de Fora. It then stops at Largo da Graça, site of the conspicuous blue Vila Sousa, the workers' village built by industrialists in the late 19th century for workers and their families. Passengers often alight here for the Miradouro da Graça , with an open-air café and great views of the castle and central Lisbon. It's particularly popular at sunset, with a glass in hand. Behind the *miradouro* the Igreja da Graça dates back to 1271, but underwent major reconstruction after the Great Earthquake.

The tram plunges down from Graça through the medieval streets of pictur-

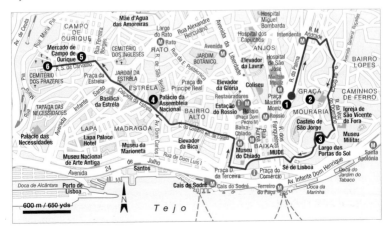

600 m / 650 yds

The tram makes its way towards Cemitério dos Prazeres

esque Alfama. One of the busiest stops is the **Largo das Portas do Sol** ❸ with a beautiful view over the red rooftops to the River Tagus. This is the most convenient stop for the castle.

BAIXA AND BAIRRO ALTO

From Largo das Portas do Sol, the tram rattles down to the Sé (Cathedral), trundles along the Rua da Conceição in the flat Baixa (lower town), then creaks its way up to the Largo do Chiado with elegant stores and the famous A Brasiliera Café just near the tram stop; next along is the nearby Praça Luís de Camões; then it's the picturesque Bairro Alto.

ESTRELA AND CAMPO DE OURIQUE

From Bairro Alto it's up and down long streets all the way to the smart district of Estrela, passing on the right the large **Palácio da Assembleia** ❹ (Parliament building) in the former São Bento Convent. Beyond it, you are unlikely to miss the huge domed **Basílica da Estrela**, where the tram stops. Many tourists alight here as this is the last major tourist site along the route. After a visit to the church (see Route 5), you can take a stroll in the delightful gardens opposite, where there is a café beside the pond.

Foodies should stay on the tram until at least the penultimate stop, Igreja

Santo Condestável, for the **Mercado de Campo de Ourique** ❺ (Rua Coelho da Rocha, Sun–Wed 10am–11pm, Thur–Sat 10am–1am), a 19th century market with a great display of fresh produce and a hip food court with gourmet stalls serving everything from suckling pig to custard tarts and flavoured gins. It's open for brunch, lunch, snacks, dinner or evening drinks – often with music or entertainment.

The tram terminus is Prazeres, where you can visit the **Cemitério dos Prazeres** ❻, the huge Prazeres Cemetery, created in 1833 after the outbreak of a cholera epidemic. It has the graves and mausoleums of many famous Portuguese.

The tram by Basílica da Estrela

Romantic Palácio da Pena

SINTRA

Known by the Romans as the Mountains of the Moon, the Serra da Sintra is a magical, palace-dotted landscape which feels as if it has sprung from a storybook. If you choose just one trip from Lisbon, make it this one.

DISTANCE: 16km (10 miles), some of which can be done on foot.

TIME: 1 or 2 full days

START: Sintra railway station

END: Sintra

POINTS TO NOTE: Sintra is 26km (16 miles) northwest of Lisbon, and is easily reached by train from Lisbon's Rossio Station (departures every 14–20 minutes, journey time 45 minutes). Trains are often very crowded. Arrive as early as possible and to avoid the worst of the crowds go straight to Pena Palace (most tourists start in the centre and hit the palace later). The Scotturb tourist Bus 434 (every 15 minutes from 9.15am) links the station, town centre, Pena Palace and Moorish Castle (see www.scotturb.com). Sintra is linked to the Quinta da Regaleira and Monserratte Palace by the less frequent Scotturb Bus 435. Tickets can be bought from the bus driver. One day bus passes for unlimited travel are available. A good day to go is a Monday, when Lisbon sights are closed but major ones in Sintra are open.

On a cool fertile highland, Sintra was long the coveted summer retreat of Portuguese royalty. Praised by generations of travellers for the beauty of its forest glades and craggy mountains, enchanting views and eccentric buildings, the town is irresistible. Lord Byron, who could find little good to say about the Portuguese, was enamoured of Sintra and likened it to 'Elysium's gates'. The Lawrence Hotel where he began writing *Childe Harold's Pilgrimage* still stands and claims to be the oldest hotel on the Iberian peninsula.

Despite the daily influx of tourists, Sintra makes a romantic getaway for visitors. Clustered throughout the forested hillsides are old palaces and estates with spectacular vistas, some as far as the sea. Two peaks in the range are crowned by reminders of Sintra's past: Castelo dos Mouros, the ruins of a castle built by the Moors in the 8th century, and Palácio de Pena, the fantasy palace built by a German nobleman for his Portuguese queen. The views from either of these points extend as far as the sea, and the entire area, thick with

vegetation and paths through the hills, provides spectacular trekking. After Lisbon it seems like another world and has its own special, cooler-than-Lisbon climate – a clash of warm southerlies and moist westerlies over the Serra da Sintra – and an almost bucolic way of life. In 1995 the Serra de Sintra was declared a Unesco World Heritage Site. It is a small area but there are 10 national monuments in the region. Ideally you should stay for two days or more, to see all the attractions.

Sintra is also accessible by car: take the IC-19 from Lisbon and follow signs for the centre when you arrive. However, note that roads in Sintra are very steep and narrow, there is a frustrating one-way system and parking is near impossible. Drivers should avoid rush-hour traffic and preferably weekends.

If you're staying in Sintra in season it's easier to leave the car at your hotel and take the buses linking the main sights. If staying the night, see page 114 for accommodation.

PALÁCIO DA PENA

From the **railway station** ❶ the Scotturb Bus No 434 heads into the centre of Sintra, which is known as **Sintra-Vila** ❷, a picturesque small town with cobbled streets and tall, pastel-washed house. It centres on the Palácio Nacional (which you will see later), distinguished from afar by its prominent twin conical chimneys. Stay on the bus while it negotiates the hairpin bends through thick woods up to **Palácio da Pena** ❸ (Pena Palace; www.parquesdesintra.pt; daily: Park: 9.30am–8pm (last ticket 7pm),

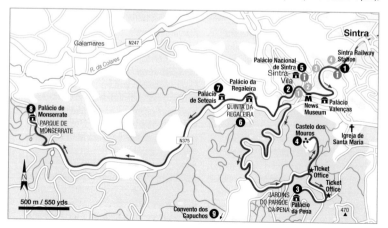

The extraordinary design of Palácio da Pena

Palace interior 9.45am–7pm, last ticket 6.15pm, low season Park and Palace 10am–6pm, last ticket 5pm).

From the main entrance you can take the shuttle bus or walk by way of a park so lush with flowering trees and vines it resembles a tropical rainforest. On the highest peak of Sintra, 450m (1,500ft) above sea-level, the palace is visible from miles around. Close at hand, it is a bizarre and extravagant pot-pourri of Gothic, Renaissance, Moorish and Manueline architecture. The exterior is a wild, layered construction painted pink (the former monastery) and yellow (the new palace), with crenellated turrets, a studded archway and monsters guarding doorways. The views from the terraces sweep all the way from the Atlantic to Lisbon. An alfresco café makes the most of them.

Palace interior

This castle of dreams and fantasy was fashioned as a love nest for Maria II and her smitten husband, Prince Ferdinand of Saxe-Coburg-Gotha (cousin of Albert, consort to Queen Victoria). Few have had the wealth to indulge their free-running fantasies quite so grandly. Rooms are full of imaginative, ornate and sumptuous detail. The original building was a Hieronymite monastery, built by Manuel I, severely damaged in the 1755 earthquake, but retaining the Manueline-style tiered cloister, decorated with patterned *azulejos* and the beautiful tiled chapel. The former monks' refectory became the dining room, and the monks' chapter house and dormitory the apartments of King Carlos. Rooms designed for the entertainment of VIP guests were the Arabic Room, with its mosque-like appearance and *trompe l'oeil* decoration, the lavishly decorated Great Hall and the Stag Room, designed in the style of a knights' banqueting hall, both rooms displaying the Palace's wonderful glass collection. Stained glass was one of Ferdinand's great passions.

Palace grounds

To complete the hedonistic experience you should go for a long stroll in the park, taking in the Valley of the Lakes, with the view from below of the Palace against the sky, the Chalet and Garden of the Countess of Edla, the Garden of the Camellias and the Temple of Columns. Above the palace, a marked footpath climbs up to the *Cruz Alta* (High Cross) which marks the highest point in the Sintra hills. (You will need the leaflet which comes with the ticket to find your way around.)

After the death in childbirth of Queen Maria II, Ferdinand married his mistress, the opera singer Elise Hensler, a Swiss-American emigrée who had trained in Paris as an opera singer. She was later made Countess Edla, but her place within the Portuguese royal court was never fully accepted and Ferdinand never cohabited with her in the palace itself. Instead they built the

Palácio Nacional de Sintra

Chalet da Condessa d'Edla or 'House of Delights', a secluded idyllic retreat within a romantic garden setting at the western end of the park. Within the gardens they introduced an exotic botanical collection with over 200 species, among them camellias, azaleas, rhododendrons and tree ferns.

CASTELO DOS MOUROS

Take the Vila Sassetti footpath (or bus) from the Pena Palace to the **Castelo dos Mouros** ❹ (www.parquesdesintra.pt; daily 9.30am–8pm, last visit 7pm; low season 10am–6pm, last visit 5pm), the Moorish castle. Restored in the 1830s, this is the oldest monument in Sintra. The dauntless Dom Afonso Hen-

Church and phone box in Sintra

rique conquered it from the Moors in 1147, a major victory in the reconquest of Portugal. A fascinating ruin, its crenellated walls hug a rocky ridge overlooking the town. The highest peak (540m/ 1,772ft) affords terrific views stretching to the sea and encompassing the entire forested area, with palaces and private *quintas* (estates) in their privileged seclusion. The mountainside is a luxuriant mass of vegetation – subtropical plants, boulders covered with moss, giant ferns, walnut, chestnut and pine trees. A delightful path zigzags its way down through the forest to Sintra-Vela via the Vila Sassetti garden – or you can use your bus ticket to return to the town.

For sustenance in Sintra-Vela centre, try the pastries at **Casa Piriquita**, see ❶, or the tapas at **Romaria de Baco**, see ❷. Then make for the national palace, dominating the centre.

PALÁCIO NACIONAL DE SINTRA

Distinctive for its twin chimneys, the **Palácio Nacional de Sintra** ❺ (National Palace; www.parquesdesintra.pt; daily 9.30am–6.30pm, low season until 5.30pm) lies in the heart of Sintra-Vela. The conspicuous chimneys were used to let the smoke out of the massive kitchen when oxen were being roasted for large banquets given for visiting dignitaries.

A summer home for Portuguese kings since the early 14th century, the palace's design became more and more unpredictable and haphazard as wings

The Swan Room's ceiling

Quinta da Regaleira's 'initiation well'

were added over the centuries, with back-to-back medieval and Manueline styles. The resulting interiors and furnishings are remarkable, including exquisite antiques from all over the world and some of the oldest and most valuable collections of *azulejos* in Portugal. The palace continued as a residence for Portuguese royalty until the fall of the monarchy in 1910.

Palace interior

The so-called **Sala dos Cisnes** (Swan Room), used for banquets and receptions was named after the ceiling panels, painted with 27 swans, all in different poses but each with a gold crown around its neck. Beyond it the **Sala das Pegas** (Magpie Salon), where notables were received, has a ceiling painted with 136 magpies. King João I (1385–1433) had the panels painted after he was caught by Queen Philippa kissing one of her ladies-in-waiting. The palace gossips had a field day until the king ordered the entire ceiling of the hall closed and painted with magpies, as many as there were magpie-like gossips. King Sebastião's room has a portrait of the monarch who led a disastrous crusade to North Africa in 1578, the Battle of the Three Kings, when nearly 15,000 were captured or killed. The royal line was weakened and two years later the Spanish annexed the Portuguese crown.

State rooms end with the striking **Sala das Basões**, its grand dome emblazoned with coats of arms of royalty and nobility and the walls adorned with blue and white tiled panels depicting hunting and bucolic scenes. The prison room has a different tale to tell. The dull-witted Afonso VI (1643–1683) was pressured into abdicating to allow his more effective brother, Pedro II, to become king. When a plot to restore Afonso to the throne was discovered, the former monarch was exiled to Sintra and imprisoned in this simple room for nine years, until he died in 1683. The visit continues via the much-restored Palatine Chapel and ends with the Arab Room with Moorish fountain and tiles.

If returning to Lisbon, it's only about a 10-minute walk to the station. Pop in to **Fábrica das Verdadeiras**, see ❸, for pastries en route, or enjoy a candlelit evening meal at **A Raposa**, see ❹, near the station. Trains back to the capital run until after midnight (www.cp.pt).

QUINTA DA REGALEIRA

On your second day in Sintra, a 20-minute walk uphill (2km/1.2 miles), a

Festival de Sintra

Sintra's lively summer festival (www.festivaldesintra.pt), held in May or June, features a series of musical events, mainly classical, which take place in historic palaces, estates and gardens in Sintra and the region.

Palácio de Monserrate

quick taxi ride or Bus 435 from the centre of Sintra will bring you to the **Quinta da Regaleira** ⑥ (www.regaleira.pt; daily Apr–Sep 10am–7pm, Feb, March and Oct 10am–6pm, Jan, Nov and Dec 10am–5pm; guided tours 6–8 times daily, book ahead), one of Sintra's oldest and grandest *quintas*. This fantastic late 19th-century multi-turreted mansion has magical and mysterious gardens speckled with follies such as the 'initiation well' which you walk down via a spiralling staircase. The palace interior was designed by an Italian theatre set designer and architect, Luigi Manini, for a millionaire Brazilian merchant, Antonio Carvalho Monteiro and his family. The exuberant mix of Manueline, Gothic and Renaissance styles would be out of place anywhere but Sintra, but it is the gardens that are the real attraction with their grottos, underground walkways, fountains and a Promenade of the Gods, with statues of nine classical gods.

PALÁCIO DE SETEAIS

Just along the road on the other side is the **Palácio de Seteais** ⑦ (www.tivoli hotels.com). *Seteais* means seven sighs, clearly a reference to the great beauty of the surroundings. The palace was turned into a luxury hotel and restaurant in 1955 but many of its original features have been preserved; it is worth seeing, if only for tea or a drink. Grand rooms are decorated with crystal chandeliers, tapestries, murals and antique furnish-

ings. From the gardens, with sculpted hedges and lemon trees, are magnificent views of the countryside – views which inspired Byron.

PALÁCIO DE MONSERRATE

Another 2.5km (1.5 miles) along the wooded road will bring you to **Palácio de Monserrate** ⑧ (www.parquesde sintra.pt; daily Mar–Oct 9.30am–7pm, Nov–Feb 10am–5pm). Take the No 435 bus or order a taxi at the hotel. This Moorish style villa, inspired by Brighton Pavilion, was built in the 19th century and set amid exotic lush gardens. After Pena Palace with all its crowds, peaceful Monserrate is a delight to visit. The first

Sun, sea and sand at Praia de Maçãs

Monserrate's interior　　　*Medieval cloister of the Convento dos Capuchos*

palace was built by Gerard de Visme, an English merchant, in 1790. The hugely wealthy English novelist, art collector and politician, William Beckford, fell in love with it and rented the palace from 1793–1799, restoring the property and constructing its first botanical garden. Half a century later Sir Francis Cook, the English textile merchant and art collector, bought the property, turned it into a romantic Moorish/Gothic folly and, with help from the head gardener of Kew Gardens, landscaped the grounds.

Lord Byron was inspired by a visit to Monserrate in 1809 and praises its beauty in *Childe Harold*. After this it became compulsory viewing for writers and artists, especially English ones, on their travels to Portugal. The gardens have a remarkable collection of species from five continents, from ornamental lakes, waterfalls and fountains to tree ferns and palm-trees as well as agaves and yuccas recreating a corner of Mexico. The palace, recently restored and reopened, reflects the eclectic spirit of the 19th century, with its Moorish-Gothic and Italian-style influences.

CONVENTO DOS CAPUCHOS

If you have a car, don't miss a visit to one of the strangest sights of the Serra: the **Convento dos Capuchos** ❾ (3.6km, just over 2 miles on the N375 from the Palácio de Monserrate or 8km [5 miles] from Sintra along the N247; www.parquesdesintra.pt; Mar–Oct 9.30am–8pm; Nov–Feb 10am–6pm; last entry one hour before closure), an atmospheric Franciscan monastery, tucked away in the woods and built entirely out of rocks and cork. There are no buses but you can walk to the monastery from Sintra, along a wooded road, or take a taxi for €35–40 return.

It was built in the 16th century but abandoned in 1834 with the suppression of the religious orders in Portugal. Small, simple and rustic, it is completely integrated into its rural surrounds, to the extent that granite boulders have been incorporated into the building. Some cells are so tiny you have to crawl through. Some say the monks lined them with cork to obtain absolute silence – but there is little noise in the forest other than birdsong. More likely, the cork helped the monks tolerate the long and humid winters.

After a visit in 1581, King Philip I of Portugal (also Philip II of Spain) stated that in all his kingdoms the two places he most preferred were El Escorial (in Spain) for its wealth and the Capuchos Convent in Sintra for its poverty.

BEACHES

The proximity of good beaches is yet another attraction of Sintra, as is the enjoyable ride on the quaint tram which departs for the coast all year (three a day in season, two in winter but no trains in Nov). The tram takes you to **Praia das Maçãs**, liveliest of the resorts on this

The village of Azenhas do Mar

coast, with seafood restaurants. The tram twists, bumps and screeches its way through some lovely scenery.

If you have a car, head for the less touristy **Praia Grande** to the south, a broad sandy beach where you can enjoy gorgeous sea and sunset views at Bar do Fundo, maybe with sushi or sea bass, washed down with *vino verde*. Or there is

lovely little **Adraga**, with soft sand, rock formations and another excellent fish restaurant. Beware though, this is the Atlantic and both beaches are pounded by Atlantic rollers. North of Praia das Maças, **Azenhas do Mar** is a lovely village clinging to the cliff face, with a small beach and natural rock seawater pools for swimming.

Food and drink

1 CASA PIRIQUITA

Rua das Padarias 1, Sintra; tel: 219 230 626; www.piriquita.pt; Thu–Tue 9am–9pm; €

Opposite the National Palace in the town centre this would be an inconspicuous café were it not for the long queues outside to buy its famous tarts. It is noisy, friendly and packed with Portuguese but worth waiting for a table or buying from the bakery. For 150 years it is has been producing scrumptious little *queijadas* (sweet cheese pastries that were used as a form of payment in medieval times) and *travesseiros* ('pillows', with a creamy almond filling). If it is a Wednesday (closing day) go to their other branch up the road, at Rua das Padarias 18.

2 ROMARIA DE BACO

Rua Gil Vicente 2, Sintra; tel: 219-243 985; www.romariadebaco.pt; daily 11am–midnight; €€

Just off the main square, this informal restaurant has a good range of tapas and *petiscos* (snacks), as well as vegetarian

dishes, salads and Portuguese meat and fish specials.

3 FÁBRICA DAS VERDADEIRAS

Volta do Duche 12, Sintra; tel: 219-230 493; daily 9am–6.30pm; €

On the road between the station and the centre, and announced by a mouthwatering aroma, this fábrica has been churning out *queijadás de Sintra* (pastries with a filling of cottage cheese, egg and sugar) for over 150 years. Try them with coffee, or perhaps a glass of port, in this small welcoming café or take them away in packs of six.

4 A RAPOSA

Rua Conde Ferreira 29; tel: 219-243 440; closed Mon; open as a café by day, restaurant in the evening; €€€

On a side street near the station, this is a beautiful dining room in an old house, offering delicious Portuguese and Mediterranean dishes. The bread is homemade and is served warm with fresh local cheese and olive oil. Impromptu *fado* may be thrown in.

Praia dos Pescadores is the main beach in Cascais

THE CASCAIS COAST

Take a trip to Lisbon's illustrious beach resorts, whose balmy climate and gracious lifestyle lured exiled royalty, nobility and spies in the last century. In summer Lisboetans escape the steamy city for the cooler Atlantic shores.

DISTANCE: train Lisbon to Estoril 26km (16 miles); walk Estoril and Cascais 4km (2.5 miles); cycle ride to Praia do Guincho 9km (5.5 miles). Driving (Lisbon to Cabo da Roca): 50km (31 miles).

TIME: A full day

START: Cais do Sodré, Lisbon

END: Cabo do Roca (or Cascais)

POINTS TO NOTE: Estoril and Cascais are linked to Lisbon by regular, inexpensive trains from Cais do Sodré, taking 30–45 minutes. Depending on time you could skip Estoril – Cascais is livelier with more attractions. A great way to get to the Guincho beaches from Cascais is to bike along the scenic coastal cycle path. Cheap, basic bikes called Bicas can be picked up opposite the Cascais train station. Alternatively hire bikes, including electric ones, from Portugal Rent Bike (Rua Alexandre Herculano, No 11, Loja 9; tel: 934-432 304; www.portugalrentbike.com). Buses go from Cascais to Praia do Guincho but the service is not sufficiently regular to depend on them for an afternoon.

West of Lisbon, and easily reached by train, this cosmopolitan playground offers first-rate hotels and restaurants, a glorious coastline, excellent sporting facilities and a history, culture and atmosphere quite unlike that of Lisbon. Beaches are very much part of the attraction, from the sands of Cascais and Estoril, teeming in high season, to the less crowded, Atlantic-battered beaches to the north. Cascais and Estoril both make excellent bases from which to explore the coastline. Hiring a car to discover the coast will obviously give you the most flexibility and get you to Cabo da Roca. If this is your preference, note that hiring in Cascais is more relaxing than contending with Lisbon traffic.

ESTORIL

Take the Cascais train from Cais do Sodré, with views of the Tagus and the Atlantic, and alight at **Estoril**. As early as the mid-18th century, this coastal town was attracting visitors for its climate and thermal spa baths. During World War II the area acquired a glamorous reputation,

Praia do Tamariz is wonderful for families

attracting an exotic community of royal refugees, among them the toppled King Umberto II of Italy, Carol II of Romania, Miklós Horthy, Regent of Hungary and Don Juan (father of Juan Carlos I of Spain).

Enjoying the breeze of neutral Portugal, German spies flocked to the Hotel Parque (torn down after the war) while their English counterparts lodged at the grander Palácio Estoril (still standing). Ian Fleming was reputedly inspired to write his first James Bond novel, *Casino Royale*, after his stay here, and the hotel served as a backdrop for scenes in the 1969 film of *On Her Majesty's Secret Service.*

Estoril is today a tourist and business resort and a place for summer homes or comfortable retirement. It may not be as grand as it used to be but it retains a certain elegance and sophistication, has gardens of palms and pines, golden (but crowded) sands and world-class golf courses.

Casino Estoril

The train station is conveniently located between the main attractions: the beach of Tamariz and the formal gardens stretching up to the modern **casino ❶** (www. casino-estoril.pt; gaming tables and slot machines 3pm–3am; ID required, gamblers must be 18 or over, no shorts, sportswear or sandals). Europe's largest casino, this is Estoril's one-stop after dark amusement centre with its nightclub, restaurants and bars, cinema, exhibition halls, shops, shows and entertainment. Gambling is suspended on only two

nights a year: Good Friday and Christmas Eve. Legend has it that somebody broke the bank one Good Friday, prompting a superstitious management to declare it a holiday thenceforth. (Officials dismiss the story as wishful thinking.)

Casino Estoril

Praia do Tamariz

Just below the bus and train stations the **Praia do Tamariz** ❷ (Tamariz Beach) buzzes all summer. With its relatively calm seas, and plentiful facilities including a string of lively bars and restaurants, it's a popular spot for Portuguese families and holiday camps. If the crowds are all too much, splash out at the new **Reverse Pool and Beach lounge** (www.reversepoolandbeach.com) where you can stretch out on a sunbed by the pool,

Praia dos Pescadores, Cascais

just above the beach, with a cool cocktail and a plate of sushi.

From Estoril you can walk to neighbouring Cascais along the attractive seaside **promenade** ❸ (15 minutes), popular with Portuguese joggers, cyclists and strollers. Cafés along the way make the most of the sea views.

CASCAIS

Known as the town of kings and fishermen, it was here that King Luís I (1838–1889) established his summer residence in the sea-view citadel. And it was in Cascais that the royal family first acquired the habit of going to the beach and bathing – not just for fun

Cascais's town square with Dom Pedro statue

but for therapeutic and medicinal purposes. The aristocracy from all over Portugal followed suit, building palaces and stately mansions, turning Cascais into a cosmopolitan resort. After the assassination of King Carlos in 1908 and the proclamation of the Republic two years later, Cascais was left in the hands of the fishermen – but not for long. In 1926, when the railway link from Lisbon became electrified, it was already becoming a seaside paradise with its golden sands, fine scenery and seafood restaurants.

Cascais is now a large and vibrant resort, retaining some elegant 19th-century villas along the coastline, good beaches and an attractive old quarter, albeit very tourist-orientated. Fishing as an industry has almost died out, though there are vestiges of the old fishing village and lobster pots piled high beside the main Praia dos Pescadores.

The town centre
The town centre has prettily cobbled pedestrian streets with cafés, restaurants and pubs spilling out on to the street and buzzing late into the night. The main focus is the Largo Luís de Camões. The alfresco cafés here have their charm, but for something less touristy, head north to the revamped market and join the Portuguese at **Marisco Na Praça**, see ❶, for arguably the best fish in town. For sea views choose **Baia do Peixe**, see ❷, or for bargain grilled spicy chicken and chips, **Somos um Regalo**,

Peacock in the park   *Casa das Histórias Paula Rego*

see ③, a 5-minute walk west from Largo Luís de Camões.

Cidadela

The cultural attractions of Cascais are all to the west of the centre. Overlooking the bay is the **Cidadela** ❹, a 17th century military fort and one of the few buildings to have survived the earthquake and tidal wave of 1755. It has been restored and is now home to a modern pousada, which manages the stylish art studios and galleries around the square and has a *taberna* serving tapas and Portuguese pastries on the square in summer. The yellow building overlooking the square is the summer residence of the President of Portugal. On the far side of the Citadela is the swish **marina**, with fancy bars, restaurants and shops.

Parque Municipal

West of the citadel is the **Parque Municipal,** a well-kept park with tropical vegetation, fountains, statues and peacocks. Overlooking a small creek, within a castle-like turreted mansion, is the **Museu Condes de Castro Guimarães** ❺ (Tue–Sun 10am–5pm, Sat–Sun 10am–1pm and 2–5pm). This was the home of the Count of Guimarães who bequeathed the mansion, along with all its antiques, paintings and porcelain, to the town in 1892.

At the north entrance of the park is the **Ecocabana**, with cheap bikes to rent and plenty of useful information and maps on the many hiking and biking routes in the region.

Casa das Histórias Paula Rego

Cross the road for the **Casa das Histórias Paula Rego** ❻ (House of Stories Paula Rego; www.casadashistoriaspaularego.com; daily Tue–Sun 10am–6pm). The museum makes a bold statement with its two terracotta towers, inspired by the chimney towers of Sintra's National Palace. It is dedicated to the Portuguese-born, London-based artist Paula Rego, Portugal's most famous female artist. The museum showcases her (often disturbing) paintings, drawings and etchings – many reflecting feminism – over 50 years of her prolific artistic career.

Museu do Mar

Just to the east is the **Museu do Mar** ❼ (Maritime Museum; Tue–Fri 10am–5pm, Sat–Sun 10am–1pm, 2–5pm) which

Estoril Music Festival

The long-established **Estoril Music Festival** (www.festorilisbon.com) sees some of the world's most prestigious chamber orchestras and soloists, but also opens the stage to young talent from across the world. The event takes place over three weeks in July and concerts are held in the Estoril Congress Centre, the Cascais Cultural Centre, Monastery of Jerónimos in Belém and other prestigious settings in Lisbon.

Surfers at Praia do Guincho

captures much of the town's fishing heritage and displays treasure recovered from sunken wrecks. This is the site of the old Sporting Club of Cascais, founded by King Carlos, where the leisured classes came for croquet, target shooting, scavenger hunts, lawn tennis matches and football (the first football match in Portugal was played here in 1888).

East of the museum is a peaceful old quarter with pretty streets around the **Igreja de Nossa Senhora da Assunção.** The plain facade of the church belies a feast of gilt and pre-earthquake *azulejos*.

PRAIA DO GUINCHO

A short drive or bracing 15-minute walk west along the seafront from Cascais will bring you to the **Boca do Inferno**

(Mouth of Hell), a geological curiosity where in rough weather the waves send up fierce fountains of spray, accompanied by ferocious sound effects. Another good reason for coming here is the **Mar do Inferno**, see ❹, for its superb seafood. In another 2.5km (1.5 miles) there is another seafood haven: the **Furnas do Guincho**, see ❺.

The N247 coastal road continues north to **Praia do Guincho** ❾ (9km/5.5 miles north of Cascais), a spectacular sweeping beach where Atlantic rollers crash on to the sands. It is a haven for professional surfers and windsurfers, hosting the Portuguese National Surfing and Body Boarding Championships. Surf shops rent out equipment, including wet suits which are recommended even in summer. Strong swells form dangerous rip tides and the waves here are not for beginners or weak swimmers. Set on the rocks, with spectacular views of the ocean, is the 5-star **Hotel Fortaleza do Guincho**, a former fort which boasts a Michelin-starred restaurant (see page 121).

CABO DA ROCA

The coast road climbs over craggy cliffs as far as windswept **Cabo da Roca** (13km, 8 miles) where cliffs drop sheer into the sea. For a fee, the tourist office here will provide you with a certificate (in antique or modern style) confirming you have reached the most westerly point of mainland Europe. A lighthouse sits at the

Sports galore

Sports enthusiasts are spoilt for choice on the Cascais coast. Top surfers come for the Atlantic rollers north of Cascais; kayaking, bodyboarding, kitesurfing and waterskiing are also popular. Estoril is a well known all-year golf resort with several courses in the surrounding area (see www.golf-portugal.net). Some hotels offer special golf holiday deals. The luxurious Palacio Estoril (see page 115) owns the famous Golf do Estoril, designed by Mckenzie Ross. Some of the most important golf tournaments have taken place here.

Lighthouse at Cabo da Roca

top of the cliffs at 140m (459ft). Beware of strong gusts of wind on the cliff edge.

If driving, return to Lisbon via the coastal road ('the Marginal') or if you crave more excitement try your luck at the Casino in Estoril (maybe with a Chinese meal at its excellent Mandarim restaurant) or disco the night away in Cascais.

Food and drink

1 MARISCO NA PRAÇA
Mercado da Vila, Cascais; tel:916-702 750; daily lunch and dinner; €€€
You won't get fish much fresher than this. It's in the new market right next door to the fish stalls and has a magnificent array of seafood to select from. Price is by kg or 100g so take care when choosing that you have a rough idea of the cost – and note the bread and olives on the table don't come free of charge! Choose from red king prawns, razor clams, sea bass, king crabs – and plenty more. Reservations advisable.

2 BAÍA DO PEIXE
Avenida Dom Carlos 1, Cascais; tel: 214-865 157; www.baiadopeixe.com; €€
This inviting fish restaurant above the Praia das Pescadores has lovely bay views from the terrace. The *Rodizio de Peixe* menu, comprising fish soup, five grilled fish, vegetables and dessert for €15.60 all in is great value. Or you could splash out on the wonderful seafood platter.

3 SOMOS UM REGALO
Avenida Vasco da Gama 36, tel: 214-865 487; www.somosumregalocascais.pt; Tue–Sun noon–3pm, 7–11pm; €
This simple *churrasqueira* is known for its *franguinho da Guia*, chicken served as spicy as you like it, barbecued to a tasty crisp, served with tomato salad, rice and chips, and washed down with sangria or a €2 euro glass of wine. Good pastries too. Expect to queue.

4 MAR DO INFERNO
Boca do Inferno, Avenida Rei Humberto II Itália, Cascais; tel: 214-832 218; www.mardoinferno.pt; closed Wed; €€€
This long-established family-run restaurant sits on the cliffs north of Cascais and offers a fabulous choice of fresh fish and seafood. Take your pick from cataplana clams, goose barnacles (tastier than they look!), sea bream, sole or large Cascais crabs. Excellent wines too – ask the staff for recommendations. Booking advisable.

5 FURNAS DO GUINCHO
Estrada do Guincho, tel: 214-869 243; www.furnasdoguincho.pt; Mon–Fri 12.30–4pm, 7.30–11pm, Sat–Sun 12.30–11pm; €€€
Watch Atlantic waves crash against the rocks while tucking into stuffed spider crab, rock lobster, shellfish paelha, fish stew Furnas-style or whole seabass baked in a salt crust. Booking is essential at this buzzing modern restaurant with its seductive setting on the rocks.

SERRA DA ARRÁBIDA

A car is essential for this trip to the spectacular and unspoilt Serra da Arrábida. The tour starts at the fishing port of Setúbal, renowned for fish restaurants, then takes in glorious beaches and rugged green hills before heading west to Sesimbra and the windswept promontory of Cabo Espichel.

DISTANCE: 185km (115.5 miles) including return journey from Lisbon
TIME: A full day
START: Setúbal
END: Cabo Espichel
POINTS TO NOTE: From Lisbon you can cross the Tagus by either bridge: the Ponte Vasco da Gama (A12) or the Ponte Abril 25 (A2), depending on your starting point. The route via Ponte Abril 25 is slightly shorter but often takes longer due to traffic congestion. Both bridges are subject to tolls. To return to Lisbon from Cabo Espichel, take the A2. For a tour of the Palácio and Quinta da Bacalhôa you need to book in advance. For the José Maria da Fonseca Winery you can usually just turn up and join a tour, but a reservation is worthwhile to be on the safe side.

The topographical highlight of the peninsula is the **Parque Natural de Arrábida**, the protected national park with a 22-mile (35km) long mountain chain that protects the coast from the strong north winds and is rich in Mediterranean vegetation. The landscape is wonderfully rugged, with wild green slopes contrasting with the intense blue of the sea. On the southern side the sea has eroded the hills and formed towering craggy cliffs and hidden sandy beaches. On the northern side are gentle rolling hills filled with vineyards.

SETÚBAL

Although **Setúbal** ❶ is an industrial town and the third largest fishing port in Portugal, it preserves a pedestrianised historic centre, a wealth of good seafood restaurants and one of the finest fish markets in Portugal. The region also produces the highly-regarded, sweet Moscatel de Setúbal wines.

The fish industry goes back centuries. If you visit the tourist office at Travessa Frei Gaspar 10, just off the main Avenida Luísa Todi, a glass floor reveals the remains of Romans tanks from a factory where fish was salted and processed into sauces and condiments. These were packed in amphorae and

The Convento da Arrábida dates back to the 16th century

exported by sea, particularly to Rome. In the early 20th century Setúbal was Portugal's number one centre for fishing, and particularly for sardines. A more recent claim to fame is as the birthplace of national hero José Mourinho.

Convento de Jesus

North of the tourist office, attractive narrow streets twist through the old town, leading off the jacaranda-shaded Largo da Misericordia. The cultural highlight of the town is the **Convento de Jesus** (northwest of the centre, currently under restoration), a glorious Manueline church whose high-arched ceiling is supported by six great twisted pillars and whose walls are decorated with fine panels of *azulejos* (tiles). One of the first examples of the Manueline style of architecture, it was built in 1490 by the same architect who later created Lisbon's famous Jerónimos Monastery. The adjoining monastery has been converted into the Museu de Cidade with Manueline paintings, archaeological finds, antiques and *azulejos*. During restoration, some of the works are on show at the **Galeria Municipal do Banco de Portugal** (Avenida Luísa Todi, 468) and the **Casa Bocage** (Rua de Edmond Bartissol, 12). At the east end of the town, you can see displays of salting, canning and agriculture at the **Museo de Trabalho.** The canneries may have closed but Setúbal is still renowned for fresh fish, so head down to the fishing port and choose from the restaurants for the catch of the day. **O Miguel,** see ❶, is a good bet.

On the south side of the Avenida Luísa Todi the **Mercado do Libramento** (Tue–Sun 7.30am–2pm) is a splendid mar-

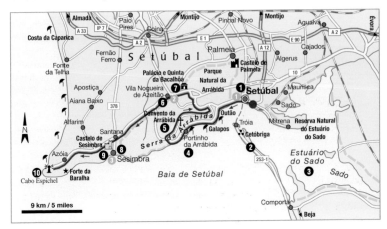

Praça do Bocage, Setubal

ket building decorated with striking blue and white *azulejos*. It has dazzling displays of fruit and vegetables, along with cheeses and hams, and a vast array of sparkling fresh fish, including whole tuna and swordfish, laid out on marble slabs. Expect to be offered delicious little bites of cheese, ham, olives and nuts – and be prepared to practice your Portuguese.

SADO ESTUARY

In summer regular ferries ply between Setúbal and the **Tróia Peninsula ❷** a long, sandy spit jutting out into the Sado estuary with popular white beaches facing the Atlantic. It is home to the luxury Tróia Resort, a 1,200 acre development with tower blocks, but you can find dense forest and unspoilt beaches and dunes further south. Tróia is said to be the site of the Roman town of Cetóbriga, destroyed by a tidal wave in the 5th century. The Roman ruins of a fish salting centre are open to the public. The unspoilt **Estuário do Sado ❸** is a haven for waders, including in spring and summer the black-winged stilt, sandpipers, and spoonbills, and in winter avocets, flamingos, cormorants, herons and plovers. The estuary is also home to a permanent colony of bottlenose dolphins, with regular **whalewatching trips** departing from Setúbal and Tróia in season. The playful bottlenose dolphins often swim alongside the boats.

ARRÁBIDA BEACHES

Take the coast road west out of Setúbal and wind your way up through woodland of pines, palms and cypresses (try to ignore the cement factory at Outão – the only sight that mars the natural beauty of the coast). Just below the road are some fabulous beaches. Beware though – these are popular beaches (particularly **Figueirinha** nearest to Setúbal) and parking in summer can be impossible unless you arrive really early. Try secluded **Galapos**, which has trickier access, hence fewer visitors. The sea is a wonderful kaleidoscope of sparkling blues and greens, and the limpid water makes for ideal snorkelling. The last of the beaches along here is **Portinho da Arrábida ❹**,

Palmela

On a spur of the wooded Serra da Arrabida, north of Setúbal, lies the attractive little hill town of Palmela. It centres around a medieval castle whose terraces offer spectacular views over the peninsula, the Sado estuary and, on a clear day, even as far as Lisbon to the north. Originally a Moorish stronghold, the castle was later expanded to incorporate a monastery. After painstaking restoration it was converted into one of Portugal's finest pousadas (see page 115). Palmela is known for its production of wine and the town hosts an annual wine festival, the Festa das Vindimas, on the first weekend of September.

The hill town of Palmela

Azeitão is known for its produce

a beautiful bathing beach of white sand. Grilled fish is the order of the day at its sleepy waterside restaurants.

ESTRADA DE ESCARPA

Shortly after Portinho da Arrábida, take the right turn (N379) with a brown sign to the **Convento da Arrábida** ❺ (tel: 212-197 620 or 932-216 552; visits on Wed, Sat and Sun only, by appointment). Above the beaches and tucked in the hills, the 16th century Franciscan monastery was resurrected as part of Lisbon University. It enjoys wonderful views of the coast and has five small chapels in the surrounding hills where the monks sought solitude. A path from the convent leads to the summit of **Formosinho**, the highest point of the Serra da Arrábida (500m), which offers expansive views and a challenging hike, taking around two hours.

From the monastery the road winds steeply up the Serra, with sensational views as you drop down the Tróia peninsula and Rio Sado. At Outão, turn left and wind your way up across the Serra to Vila Fresca Azeitão.

AZEITÃO

A cluster of small *aldeias* or villages, prosperous **Azeitão** is known for red wine, olives and creamy sheep's cheese. The olive groves gave the region the name of Azeitão, meaning 'large olive tree'. From Vila Fresca de Azeitão, follow signs for **Vila Nogueira de Azeitão** ❻,

sometimes simply called Azeitão. The villages are also known for patisserie, so recharge the batteries with a *bica* (an *espresso*) and the famous *torta de Azeitão*, a soft sponge roll filled with egg cream and cinnamon. Try the café just opposite the **Casa Museu José Maria de Fonseca** (see below); they also sell the delicious Azeitão cheese, an unpasteurised sheep's milk cheese produced in small rounds. It is still produced by a few families in artisan dairies. Or if it's time for lunch, try **Casa das Tortas**, see ❷, a couple of minutes' walk from the winery on the Praça da República.

Wineries

Large black barrels in the centre of town herald the wine cellars of the famous José Maria da Fonseca Winery, founded in 1834. The winery today still remains a family business (now in its 7th generation) and produces the soft rich Periquita, Portugal's oldest table wine – as well as Setúbal's popular dessert Moscatel wines. The main building of the winery is a 19th century mansion, which was the Fonseca family residence. The **Casa Museu José Maria da Fonseca** (Rua José Augusto Coelho, 11-13; tel: 212-198 940; www.jmf.pt; Apr–Oct daily 10am–noon, 2.30–5.30pm, Nov–Mar 10am–noon, 2.30–4.30pm) has guided tours in English, French and Spanish as well as Portuguese, providing an insight into the history of the company, the origin of Periquita and a visit to the Moscatel cellar, whose hallowed vault stores wines

Wine barrels in a cellar decorated with antique azulejos, Bacalhôa Vinhos de Portugal

that are over a 100 years old. You won't be tasting these particular ones, but you do get a chance to sample red Fonseca wine and 20 year-old Moscatel. Should you miss out on a tour you can sample wines at the **Loja de Vinhos,** the large wine shop which has longer opening hours and tastings from €1–10 a glass.

Just over 2km (1.25km) northeast on the N10 lies the **Bacalhôa Vinhos de Portugal ❼**, with a museum and winery (www.bacalhoa.com; daily 10am–6pm; 1hr tour, min 2 people, bookings recommended). A visit here can be combined with the **Palácio Bacalhôa** (Bacalhôa Palace; closed Sun, 1hr tour, recommended hours 10.30am, 2.30pm, 3.30pm). The two together only cost €6. This is one of the biggest wineries in Portugal, producing reds, whites, rosés and sparkling wines, but a visit is about art just as much as wine. The owner of the estate is José Berardo, the owner of the collection of modern art in the Museu Coleção Berardo (see page 64). As well as learning about wine processing and tasting wines you can see stunning exhibitions of African art, Art Nouveau and Art Deco, contemporary sculpture and *azulejos* spanning 500 years.

The Bacalhôa Palace, which is 3km (2 miles) away, was built in 1480 and the architecture, decor and gardens reflect the tastes of various owners who drew inspiration from their travels across Europe, Africa and the Orient. There are beautiful *majolica azulejos* panels from the 16th century and the lakeside house

has a tiled panel showing *Susanna and the Elders* dated 1565, believed to be the earliest known panel in Portugal.

SESIMBRA

16kms (10 miles) westwards along the N379 brings you to **Sesimbra ❽**, a bustling fishing port and beach resort. This is a favourite destination with the Portuguese and the outskirts have seen major development. Locals flock here at weekends and holidays for superb seafood, late nights out and the sandy beach, sheltered (in summer at least) from the brunt of Atlantic tides and harsh winds.

The beach is divided into two by the restored 17th century **Fortaleza de Santiago**, home to the tourist office and the **Museu Maritimo** (Tue–Sun summer 3.30–7pm and 8.30–11pm, off season 10am–1pm, 2.30–5.30pm) dedicated to local fishing traditions through the centuries. Quench your thirst at the Tap House with local craft beer or try the Fragoleto natural ice creams.

The catch of the day is served in the many excellent seafood restaurants, including **Casa Mateus**, see ❸, just inland. A speciality of Sesimbra is *arroz de marisco*, a shellfish and rice dish that is ideal for sharing.

The local fishing boats set out from the **Porto di Abrigo** at the far western end of the town and bring home their daily catch to be auctioned to restaurateurs. Visitors can join a guided tour to the auction on Tuesdays and Thursday

Crowds packing out Sesimbra's beach

afternoons (book at the tourist office) though there is nothing to stop you going independently. It's a noisy and absorbing affair with buyers and spectators watching large trays of the announced fish glistening on conveyor belts.

Castelo de Sesimbra

Silhouetted on the hilltop above Sesimbra and signed from the main road is the recently restored **Castelo de Sesimbra** ❾ (Sesimbra Castle; 7am–8pm, until 7pm in winter; free). During the Middle Ages the town was located here, protected against sea raiders by its walls and altitude. The Moors built the enclave, lost it to King Afonso Henriques in 1165, and won it back again for a few years before having to move out permanently in 1200. Take a look inside the **Church of Our Lady of the Consolation of the Castle** (daily; free) within the outer fortifications. It was rebuilt during the 18th century and the walls are covered with *azulejos* from floor to ceiling. The view down to the curve of the coast and back to the Arrábida mountains is magnificent.

Cabo Espichel

The Arrábida peninsula ends dramatically with the cliffs of **Cabo Espichel** ❿, 11km (7 miles) west of Sesimbra. This windswept promontory with its lighthouse and stunning sea views is also the site of the 17th-century sanctuary of **Nossa Senhora do Cabo**, decorated with a *trompe l'oeil* ceiling, Baroque paintings and decorative tiles. This used to be an impor-

tant pilgrimage site. From here it's about 50km (31 miles) back to Lisbon, going via the A2 and the Ponte 25 de Abril.

Food and drink

❶ O MIGUEL

Rua da Saude 16 and 18; tel: 265-573 332; daily for lunch and dinner; €€
Setúbal has plenty of good fish restaurants and this one, by the fishing harbour, ranks among the best. Try *dourada* (gilt-head bream), *robalo* (seabass) or *chocos fritos* (deep-fried cuttlefish), washed down with very affordable Setúbal wines.

❷ CASA DAS TORTAS

Praça da Republica 37; tel: 969-146 996; €€
Come for simply grilled fish and meat dishes and follow on with speciality *tortas* (cakes) from Azeitão with a glass of local *moscatel*. In summer, sit at trestle tables on the tree-shaded terrace. Good value.

❸ CASA MATEUS

Largo Anselmo Braancamp 4; tel: 963-650 939; www.casamateus.pt; Tue–Sun noon–3.30pm, 7–11pm; €€€
This small, sought-after seafood restaurant, near the beach and fort, has been in the same family for nearly 100 years. Come for cuttlefish, seafood curry, fish stew or grouper with clams, and be sure to leave room for delicious desserts. Reservations (inside or out) are advisable.

MAFRA AND ERICEIRA

A fascinating trip from Lisbon, either by bus or by car, this tour takes in the monumental Palace-Convent of Mafra and a visit to Ericeira, superb for seafood and surf beaches and with a delightful fishing village at its core.

DISTANCE: Lisbon to Mafra 44km (27.5 miles), Mafra to Ericeira 10km (6 miles)
TIME: Full day
START: Lisbon
END: Ericeira
POINTS TO NOTE: A car gives you more flexibility for this route, but you can also travel by bus. The service, operated by Mafrense (www.mafrense.pt), departs from Lisbon's Campo Grande terminal (served by Campo Grande Metro station). Buses marked 'Ericeira via Mafra' depart from stands 4 and 5 at least once an hour, more in peak season, taking 40 or 90 mins. Tickets are purchased from the driver. The bus stops in front of the main entrance to Mafra National Palace and continues to Ericeira. By car, the quickest route to Mafra is north along the A8; at junction 5, turn off west on to the A21 (signed Malveira/Mafra/Ericeira), taking exit 3 for the palace. Both are toll roads but the journey is only about half an hour. Mafra palace is free on the first Sunday of the month.

Mafra is a name shared by both a small modest town and a grandiose palace-convent of staggering dimensions. This 18th century architectural masterpiece was created by João V to celebrate the awaited birth of his first child, Princess Dona Maria. When originally built it was intended as a modest Franciscan monastery, but it soon morphed into a lavish palace and basilica. Such magnificence was possible due to the influx of gold from Brazil which allowed the monarch to commission top architects, sculptors and artists, many from Italy. During the reign of the king's son, José I, an important school of sculpture was founded here.

PALÁCIO NACIONAL DE MAFRA

Rising like a dark mirage across the plain stands the colossal **Palácio Nacional de Mafra ❶** (www.palacio mafra.pt; daily 9.30am–5.30pm, last admission 4.45pm; Basilica, Religious Art Museum and Infirmary can be seen separately at reduced cost, but closed 1–2pm), which is almost as large as

Palácio Nacional de Mafra

Spain's El Escorial. Work began in 1717 and drew in a 50,000-strong army of labourers, artists and craftsmen to work on its 1,000 odd rooms.

It was in the palace that the last king of Portugal, Manuel II, spent his last night before leaving for exile in October 1910, following the proclamation of the Republic. The palace was opened to the public the following year. Most of the finest furniture and paintings were taken to Brazil when João V fled from the French invasion in 1807, but there's an extensive collection of religious and historical works of art including, in the Destinies Room, a graphic allegorical painting of the Duke of Wellington returning the nation to the king after its liberation from France.

The guided tour lasts some 90 minutes and takes you from the apartments of the King at one end of the palace through the splendid Baroque library, great domed basilica and plainer quarters such as the pharmacy, long galleries and corridors, to the Queen's apartments at the other end – some 250m (800ft) away from the King's apartments!

Basilica

The facade is a massive 220 metres (720ft) long. The central point of the

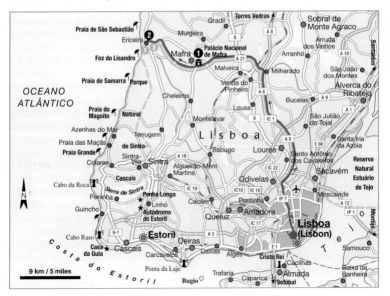

In Mafra's spectacular library

main facade is the **Basilica**, flanked by two tall towers and built in Italian Baroque style. The bell towers boast the world's largest collection of bells which can be heard for 24km (15 miles) when they are played on Sunday afternoons. The story goes that the king was informed that a single carillon of 49 bells would cost him 400,000.00 *réis*, an astronomical price for a country as small as Portugal. Offended by the suggestion, he replied 'So cheap? I'll take two!' Hence two carillons and 98 bells in all.

The basilica interior contains outstanding Portuguese and Italian sculpture, including 14 large statues of saints in the vestibule, carved from

Mass at the Basilica of Mafra Palace

Carrara marble. The church is unique in that it has six working organs, built at the same time and conceived to play together like an ensemble. Superb concerts are held here one the first Sunday of the month in summer, allowing visitors to hear the organs being played.

Rococo library

Mafra's **library**, one of the most important in Europe, is full of Rococo splendour and light. The hugely wealthy João V sent ambassadors across Europe to bring back precious collections of books. There are well over 38,000 volumes, among them a 16th century Bible in five different languages, first editions of the great epic, *Os Lusíadas* by Camões and the earliest edition of *Homer* in Greek. Only researchers, historians and scholars are allowed access to the books. The library has been beautifully preserved, thanks in part to a colony of little bats behind the shelves who keep out book-eating insects – they have been here since the 18th century!

The Infirmary and state rooms

Beyond the simple monks' cells is the **Infirmary**, the main room of the convent, a church with 16 private sickrooms lining the nave so that patients could hear mass from their beds. Reserved for the most poorly of patients, the hospital had direct access to the cemetery. It is one of

The whitewashed streets of Ericeira

only four 18th century infirmaries still in existence. The Infirmary is followed by sumptuous state rooms, including the Throne Room, with frescoes and an ornate coffered ceiling, where official audiences with the king were held. In the South Tower, the Queen's Bedroom is of historic interest, for this is where the last king of Portugal, Manuel II, slept the night before sailing off into exile in Twickenham in 1910. A portrait of the king stands on an easel at the foot of the bed.

For lunch you could choose from cafés or restaurants in Mafra, but Ericeira is a better bet with its choice of seafood.

ERICEIRA

The coastal resort and fishing village of **Ericeira ❷** lies 10km (6 miles) northwest of Mafra. The quickest route by car is via the A21 but to avoid tolls you can take the slightly longer N116. Buses depart from just outside the palace.

With its 11km (7 miles) of beaches and first-class seafood restaurants, Ericeira sees an ever-increasing influx of Portuguese and foreign visitors, along with modern development on the outskirts. But fishing traditions carry on and at its heart is an enchanting old town. If you're coming by car, head for the seafront and park in the Largo de San Sebastião. Walking along the front southwards you'll come to the **Fishermen's Port** where the day's catch is sold in the afternoon (no access for public). Keeping watch over the fishermen's beach is the **Capela de Santo António** (also known as the Chapel of our Lady of Safe Journeys). Every inch of this little chapel is tiled with blue and yellow *azulejos*. Outside, old-timers sit on tiled benches and watch the world go by. For centuries the bell and lantern which guided fishermen at night and in times of fog and storm were kept outside the church. A tiled panel here records, with some disdain, the historic event when King Manuel II boarded the royal yacht with his family from this little port to sail off into exile in the UK.

Old Quarter

Sloping up from the seafront, the fishermen's village is a picturesque quarter of cobbled, pedestrianised streets, sparkling white houses with blue-framed windows and doors and tiled panelled scenes invoking divine protection against natural catastrophes.

For lunch options there are inviting *tascas*, *marisqueiras* (seafood specialists) or small bars with signs outside saying '*ha caracois*' (we have snails). Above the **Praia dos Pescadores** (Fishermen's beach) the simple **Mar à Vista**, see ➊, serves up great shellfish or try **Mar d'Areia**, see ➋, near the fish market. After lunch walk a little way east for **Praça da República**, the lively main square with benches shaded by plane trees and surrounded by shops and cafés.

Unspoilt, wild coast near Ericeira

Surfing mecca

At the far end of Praça da República, the **tourist office** has a fascinating new interpretive centre for Europe's first surfing reserve – only the second in the world. Ericeira has had a strong surfing community since the 1960s and championships have been held here since 1977. It is one of the rare places that brings together a variety of high quality waves for all levels of surfer, at all times of the year. The exhibition has an interactive table with projectors showing the motions of the waves; on the walls are descriptions of the reef breaks, and the waves they hold. There are videos of seven types of waves, showing their comparative speed and danger. Ericeira's queen wave – and arguably the best in Portugal – is the long, fast and furious Coxos next to São Lourenço beach. Since attaining reserve status, this stretch of the coast and its flora and fauna are now protected.

The Mafrense bus will take you back to Lisbon. Driving via the A21 and A8 takes 45 minutes or more dependent on traffic.

Food and drink

① MAR À VISTA

Rua de Santo António 16, Ericeira; tel: 261-862 928; Thur–Mon noon–10pm; €€

Small and family-run, this authentic *marisqueira* has wonderful fresh shellfish. Come for *percebes* (goose barnacles), crab, clams, lobster or seafood cataplana. It's very popular, particularly with Portuguese, and it's worth booking a table.

② MAR D'AREIA

Rua da Fonte do Cabo 49, Ericeira; tel: 261-862 222; Tue–Sun lunch and dinner; €€

Tucked away in a side street and full of locals, you can always be assured here of the freshest of fish, straight from the trawlers. It's simple and friendly, run by the same family for 65 years. Pick your fish and see it sizzling on the grill before being served with a simple salad and boiled potatoes. Follow on with home-made dessert.

A surfer rides the waves at Ericeira

Queluz Palace

QUELUZ PALACE

An easy half-day outing by train to a sumptuous pink palace and gardens with Versailles-style grandeur. The royal residence illustrates the evolution in Court tastes in the 18th and 19th century, from Baroque to Rococo and Neoclassicism.

DISTANCE: 14km (9 miles) by train from Lisbon, plus 1km (0.6 mile) on foot from the station
TIME: Leisurely half-day from Lisbon
START: Rossio Station, Lisbon
END: Queluz
POINTS TO NOTE: Queluz takes less than 20 minutes on the very frequent Sintra trains from Rossio. Take the Sintra train from Rossio Station and alight at Queluz-Belas. Exit the station on the left side, ie. where the train pulls in. Follow the signs to the palace (1km/0.6 mile, via Av. António Enes and Av. República). Tickets are available for the grounds only, or you can buy a combined ticket for the palace and grounds. For a meal at Cozinha Velha, book a table in advance.

Originally conceived as a summer retreat, Queluz became the royal family's favourite palace for leisure and entertainment. They lived here from the mid-18th century until their departure for Brazil in 1807, at the time of the French invasions. Queluz had its heyday during the reign of the serious and devout Maria I (1777–99), but she suffered serious bouts of depression which deepened into madness when her son José died of smallpox.

PÁLACIO NACIONAL DE QUELUZ

The town is unprepossessing and the entrance facade is slightly shabby, but modesty is totally abandoned inside the **Palácio Nacional de Queluz** (www.parquesdesintra.pt; Apr–Oct 9am–7pm, last ticket 6pm, Nov–Mar 9am–6pm, last ticket 5pm). Though the palace lost much to French invasions (it was used by General Andoche Junot as his headquarters during the Peninsular War) and to a fire in 1934, it manages to preserve the air of 18th–19th century royal privilege and luxury.

Palace interior

The lavish **Throne Room**, once the scene of balls and banquets, is adorned with colossal chandeliers, mirrors and gilt-layered walls and ceilings. Beyond

The ornate Throne Room

it the **Music Room** was the setting for operas, concerts and plays. Some of the concerts were performed here by the Queen's orchestra which according to English traveller, William Beckford, was the best in Europe. Summer concerts are still sometimes held here. The royal family's living rooms open out onto the immaculate Malta Gardens.

Next along is the **Corredor das Mangas** (Corridor of the Sleeves) with panels of *azulejos* dating from 1784 representing the continents and seasons as well as hunting scenes and depictions of everyday life. Continue on to the **Sala dos Embaixadores** (Hall of Ambassadors) which has a floor like a chessboard, in addition to a wealth of mirrors and a *tromp l'oeil* ceiling showing the royal family attending a concert.

The final room is the **Don Quixote Chamber**, the royal bedroom, where Pedro IV, King of Portugal and first Emperor of Brazil, was born and died (1834). He was 9 when he left Queluz with his family for Brazil during the Napoleonic invasion. A liberal-minded, charismatic and ambitious man, his life was always divided between Portugal and Brazil. He was perceived in Brazil as Portuguese,

yet in Portugal was seen as a foreigner. He left numerous descendants both inside and outside of wedlock. The name of the room comes from the paintings which are based on Don Quixote's life.

Palace gardens

The palace gardens are the pride of Queluz and seem never-ending with clipped hedges in perfect geometric array, ponds, lakes and fountains, pavilions and armies of statues. The huge old magnolia trees and orange trees close by relieve some of the formality. The grounds were the setting for royal family parties, with guests entering the

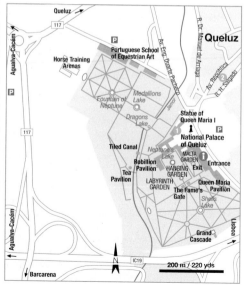

In Queluz's palace gardens   *Escadaria dos Leões*

gardens via the pompous but original **Escadaria dos Leões** (Lions' Staircase). A stream, whose retaining walls are covered in *azulejos*, was diverted to pass through the palace grounds; the sluice gates closed so that the canal filled with water and the royal guests could view the tiled scenes from a boat. In the early 19th century, dozens of live animals – not just dogs, but lions and wolves – were boarded at Queluz, which was then the site of the royal zoo.

The palace and gardens make a spectacular setting during August and September for *Noites de Queluz* (Nights at Queluz), enchanting musical recreations from the 18th century which bring the palace and gardens back to life.

Statue in the palace gardens

Eating in the palace

Separate from the main building are the ancient kitchens, now the setting of the enticing **Cozinha Velha**, see ❶, the restaurant run by the Pousada opposite the palace. For something cheaper and more local, try the **Retiro da Mina**, see ❷, nearby, on the Avenida da República across the road from the palace.

Food and drink

❶ COZINHA VELHA

Palácio Nacional de Queluz, Largo Palácio; tel: 214-356 158; daily 1–3pm, 7.30–10pm; €€€

Within the former kitchens of the palace, this handsome restaurant retains – among other features – the old stone chimney and vaulted ceiling. Expect salt cod dishes, clams cataplana, octopus or lobster salad and Chateaubriand. Be sure to leave space for the famous dessert buffet.

❷ RETIRO DA MINA

Avenida da República 10, Queluz; tel: 214-352 978; closed all day Tue and Mon dinner; €

Near the palace, this is a friendly, no-frills restaurant popular with locals and offering great value. Come for grilled squid, salted cod, whole fresh fish or a barbecued half chicken with chips and salad. Wash it down with incredibly cheap house wine – or choose a bottle from the wine list.

DIRECTORY

Hand-picked hotels and restaurants to suit all budgets and tastes, organised by area, plus select nightlife listings, an alphabetical listing of practical information, a language guide and an overview of the best books and films to give you a flavour of the city.

The fabulous terrace at Memmo Alfama

ACCOMMODATION

The most appealing places to stay are found in the city centre, while the newer, more bland hotels (many with business facilities) are further out of town. Here you get more for your euros but the sheer convenience of being near the centre, in a city of hills, is worth a lot. The hotel scene has been burgeoning in recent years with the opening of dozens of new hotels, many of them upmarket or chic boutique hotels. Prices are steadily increasing, but Lisbon is still good value compared with most cities in western Europe.

In high season (June to September) rooms are at a premium, and you should book well ahead. Given the warm climate, spring and late autumn can be busy too, but in mid-winter prices can fall substantially. If you arrive on spec head for one of the tourist offices (see page 130) who will help you find accommodation. The official tourist board hotel reservation website is www.bookinglisboa.com.

Many hotels charge extra for breakfast. Check when you make a reservation. Charges can be high (eg. €17 per person for a four star hotel) and many visitors prefer to go the local café for coffee and croissants.

City Tourist Tax – Be prepared for the city tax, introduced in 2016, for those staying overnight in the capital. The charge is €1 per adult per night, subject to a maximum of seven nights, but not applicable to children under 14. The tax is not included on the rates advertised on hotel booking websites and is charged directly to the guest at the hotel.

Alfama

Albergaria Senhora do Monte
Calçada do Monte 39; tel: 218-866 002; tram: 28; €€
The steep climb up from the centre, to the top of the highest of Lisbon's hills, is worth it for one of the finest views in the city. The modern (if a tad dated) guest rooms vary considerably in size; it's worth paying the extra for a balcony.

The Keep
Costa do Castelo 74; tel: 218-854 070; www.thekeep-lisbon.com; bus 737; tram 28; €
This cheap guest house close to the castle offers basic accommodation and is not for the faint-hearted – you need to negotiate not only Alfama's cobbled streets but also the building's spiral staircase. The rewards are wonderful: a

> Price for a double room with breakfast for one night in high season, including service and VAT, but excluding city tourist tax:
> €€€€ = over 270 euros
> €€€ = 180–270 euros
> €€ = 100–180 euros
> € = under 100 euros

'Tribe' room at the Internacional Design Hotel

romantic flower-filled terrace with great views. No credit cards.

Memmo Alfama Design Hotel

Travessa das Merceeiras 27; tel: 210-495 660; www.memmohotels.com; tram 28; €€€

Expertly converted from a former bakery, the charming Memmo Alfama was the first boutique hotel in the Alfama. It is a stylish blend of old and new, and has a terrace with small pool and bar offering spectacular river views.

Palácio Belmonte

Páteo Dom Fradique 14; tel: 218-816 600; www.palaciobelmonte.com; bus 737, tram 28; €€€€

Built into the battlements of the castle with stunning views over the Alfama and River Tagus, this is Lisbon's oldest palace. It is also a very discreet, tranquil hotel with 11 sensational suites, a black marble pool and lush garden. The building has been beautifully restored and is adorned with panels of *azulejos* from the 1700s, period paintings and contemporary works of art.

Santiago de Alfama

Rua de Santiago 10-14; tel: 213-941 616; www.santiagodealfama.com; €€€€

This little 5-star boutique hotel, converted from a palace, has fine views of the historic Alfama and the River Tagus from upper floors. It has 19 well-equipped guest rooms, a ground floor café and a good restaurant with modern Portuguese cuisine.

Solar do Castelo

Rua das Cozinhas 21; tel: 218-806 050; www.solardocastelo.com; tram 28; €€€€

This gem of a hotel, within the walls of the castle, has just 14 rooms and an inner courtyard and garden. It's so peaceful only the peacocks are likely to waken you. Breakfast are generous. It's a steep climb from the centre – or an easy taxi ride.

Solar dos Mouros

Rua do Milagre de Santo António 6; tel: 218-854 940; www.solardosmouroslisboa.com; bus 737 or tram 28; €€€

This stylish boutique hotel up near the castle enjoys panoramic views over the River Tagus and city. There are just 13 rooms, individually designed in contemporary style with bold colours, African art and striking modern paintings.

Baixa

Internacional Design Hotel

Rua da Betesga 3; tel: 213-240 990; www.idesignhotel.com; metro: Rossio; €€€

This emphatically designer hotel, in a great location overlooking Rossio, has four types of highly conceptualised, spectacular rooms: Urban, Tribe, Zen and Pop – with magazine looks and every comfort.

Hotel Métropole

Praca Dom Pedro IV 30; tel: 213-219 030;

An upmarket room at the Four Seasons

www.almeidahotels.pt; metro: Rossio; €€
This classic 1920s hotel is centrally located right on Rossio square. It's rather faded in parts but prices are good given the location. Rooms are individually styled and the upper ones, some with private balcony, have good views over Rossio with the castle in the distance.

Pestana CR7
Rua do Comércio, 54, tel: 210-401 710; www.pestanacr7.com; metro: Terreiro do Paço; €€€€
Football fans will be flocking to this new hip hotel in downtown Lisbon, a joint venture between Cristiano Ronaldo and the Pestana hotel chain. Football themes predominate and multifunctional designer guest rooms have 48" smart HD TVs, Apple TV, USB socket chargers, yoga exercise mats and mood lighting.

Pestana Pousada Lisboa
Praça do Comércio, 31-34; tel: 210-407 640; www.pestana.com; metro: Terreiro do Paço; €€€
Lisbon's pousada has a prime location, comfortable classic rooms and attentive service. It also has an excellent restaurant and meals can be taken under the vaults in the restaurant or outside with fine views of the square.

Turim Terreiro do Paço Hotel
Rua do Comércio 9; tel: 210-330 800; www.turim-hotels.com; metro: Terreiro do Paço; €€

This hotel has a handy location just north of the main Praça do Comércio. Staff are really friendly, double glazing is highly effective, and rooms are new and modern, but very short on space.

Avenida da Liberdade/ North Lisbon

Avenida Palace
Rua 1 de Dezembro 123, tel: 213-218 100; www.hotelavenidapalace.pt; metro: Rossio; €€€€
Situated on Rossio, the remodelled Avenida Palace is one of Lisbon's finest luxury hotels. Built in 1892 it has a magnificent, old-fashioned elegance, with sumptuous public rooms and beautiful, classically-decorated guest rooms. Sybarites can opt for the Louis XVI-style room.

Britania
Rua Rodrigues Sampaio 17; tel: 213-155 016; www.heritage.pt; metro: Avenida; €€
One of Lisbon's most charming and intimate hotels, this 1940s townhouse, alongside the main Avenida da Liberdade, has been lovingly restored with genuine Art Decor touches. The rooms are spacious and elegantly appointed, with marble bathrooms.

Corinthia Hotel Lisbon
Avenida Columbano Bordalo Pinheiro 105; tel: 217-236 363; www.corinthia.com/en/ hotels/lisbon; metro: Jardim Zoológico; €€€
This 5-star hotel is a peaceful and styl-

Dive in to the Four Seasons' pool

ish sanctuary after a busy day of sightseeing. Luxe décor, live music in the Tempus Bar, a sumptuous ESPA spa and second-to-none service make the Corinthia stand out. Executive Club access available. Facilities include an indoor pool and gym, Tipico restaurant for Portuguese specialities and the glamorous Terrace Bar for cocktails.

Dom Pedro Palace

Avenida Engenheiro Duarte Pacheco 24; tel: 213-896 600; www.dompedro.com; metro: Marquês de Pombal; €€€

A swish 5-star hotel, the Dom Pedro has 23 floors of guest rooms and some spectacular views of the city. Popular with American tourists and European business travellers, it has a top-flight Italian restaurant, a bistro-style café, indoor pool, a beauty and fitness centre, and is a stone's throw from the famous Amoreiras Shopping Centre.

Epic Sana Lisboa Hotel

Avenida Engenheiro Duarte Pacheco 15; tel: 211-597 300; www.lisboa.epic. sanahotels.com; metro: Marquês de Pombal or Parque; €€€

This 5-star contemporary hotel with infinity rooftop pool and large spa and fitness centre is slightly out of the centre in Amoreiras, but you can walk to the metro in 13 minutes or take a taxi to the centre.

Ever Lisboa

Avenida da Liberdade 189; tel: 213-522 618; www.everlisboahotel.com; metro: Avenida; €€

A small, historic hotel right on the main boulevard, this 19th-century, Venetian-style former palace has a spectacular spiral staircase with a mural of Lisbon and period touches such as stained-glass windows. Rates are reasonable given the location.

Expo Astória

Rua Braamcamp 10; tel: 213-861 317; www.expoastoria.pt; metro: Marquês de Pombal; €

This attractive Art Deco hotel has spacious rooms and is just a minute's walk from Praça de Marquês de Pombal, with its metro station. Staff are courteous, breakfasts are good and given the location, it ranks as a bargain.

Florida Hotel

Rua Duque de Palmela 34; tel: 213-576 145; www.hotelflorida.lisbonhotels.it; metro: Marquês de Pombal; €€

The Florida is quite a quirky hotel with decor inspired by 1950s and 60s movies, and a restaurant called 'The Great American Disaster'. Some rooms are small and it's a little north of the centre, but prices are good for a 4-star, breakfasts above average and staff friendly.

Four Seasons Hotel Ritz Lisboa

Rua Rodrigues da Fonseca 88; tel: 213-814 400; www.fourseasons.com/lisbon; metro: Marquês de Pombal; €€€€

The utilitarian 1950s building belies a swanky hotel which provides the height

Chic style at the Bairro Alto Hotel

of indulgence. The 282 deluxe rooms all have marble bathrooms, views over the green Parque Edward VII and most have a private terrace. The hotel boasts a gastronomic restaurant, sushi lounge, state-of-the-art spa and Sodashi treatment menu.

Inspira Santa Marta

Rua de Santa Marta 48; tel: 210-440 900; www.inspirahotels.com; metro: Avenida or Marquês do Pombal; €€€

Near the Avenida da Liberdade, this designer hotel has admirable eco-credentials – it uses green technology, runs according to sustainable policies and supports charitable projects. Rooms and spa are modelled around *feng shui* principles.

Lisboa Palace

Travessa do Salitre 7; tel: 213-218 218; www.lisbonplazahotel.com; metro: Avenida; €€€

Off Avenida Liberdade, on a quiet street, the charming Lisboa Palace opened in the 1950s and has been in hands of the same family ever since. It has comfortable traditional rooms and very accommodating staff. Generous breakfasts too.

Porto Bay Liberdade

Rua Rosa Araújo, 8; tel: 210-015 700; www.portobay.com; metro: Marquês de Pombal; €€€

This new 5-star hotel, converted from three early 20th century palaces, preserved its historic facade but inside all is modern and the 98 comfortable rooms come complete with USB chargers, 40 inch Smart TVs and pillow menu. It's well equipped, with indoor pool, gym and spa.

Tivoli Lisboa

Avenida da Liberdade 185; tel: 213-198 900; www.tivolihotels.com; metro: Avenida; €€€

One of Lisbon's largest and longest-running luxury hotels, the Tivoli is right on the main thoroughfare, close to top designer stores. It excels in services and facilities which include the noted rooftop restaurant and heated outdoor swimming pool, tree-shaded garden and tennis court.

Valverde

Avenida da Liberdade 164; tel: 210-940 300; www.valverdehotel.com; metro: Avenida; €€€

Ideally situated for shopaholics on the elegant Avenida da Liberdade, this charming hotel has antique prints and art, fine fabrics and retro furnishings. The ground floor Sítio restaurant, with excellent Portuguese cuisine, overlooks the courtyard. Staff are delightful, and there's a heated pool and fitness centre.

VIP Executive Éden

Praça dos Restauradores 24; tel: 213-216 600; www.viphotels.com; metro: Restauradores; €€€

In a famous Art Deco ex-cinema, this cool, modern apartment-hotel is excel-

Porto Bay Liberdade suite with balcony

lent value, especially for families. There are kitchen-equipped studios, full apartments, a panoramic pool, a terrace bar and breakfast service.

Bairro Alto/Chiado/Príncipe Reale

Bairro Alto Hotel

Praça Luís de Camões 2; tel: 213-408 288; www.bairroaltohotel.com; tram 28; €€€€

Ultra-chic, this 5-star boutique hotel in the Bairro Alto has 55 rooms in six different categories, an excellent restaurant, the fashionable BA café-bar with nightly music and the top-floor BA Terrace overlooking the river and rooftops – a great spot for lunch, afternoon cocktails or a candlelit drink.

Hotel Borges Chiado

Rua Garrett 108; tel: 210-456 400; www.hotelborges.com; metro: Baixa-Chiado; €€

This typical old Lisbon hotel has plenty of character and a great location, right by the metro and close to the restaurants and elegant shops of the Chiado. Some rooms have balconies. Choose higher up ones to avoid street noise.

Hotel do Chiado

Rua Nova do Almada, 144; tel: 213-256 100; www.hoteldochiadolisbon.com; metro: Baixa-Chiado; €€€

This 4-star has a perfect location in the heart of Lisbon, with excellent shopping and a great choice of eateries nearby, plus one of the best rooftops in the city.

Rooms are furnished in contemporary style and vary in price depending on whether you have a terrace and view.

Lx Boutique Hotel

Rua Do Alecrim, 12; tel: 213-474 394; www.lxboutiquehotel.com; metro: Cais do Sodré; €€

Fashionable little boutique hotel, with chic rooms and arty themes. Guest rooms come with all modern amenities including iPod docks – the best ones overlook the river across the rooftops. The bar/lounge becomes a sushi, salad and tapas restaurant from 12.30–2pm and every afternoon, complimentary sushi is served.

Memmo Príncipe Real

Rua Dom Pedro V, 56; tel: 213-514 368; www.memmohotels.com; metro: Rato; €€€€

In the bohemian enclave of Príncipe Real, this new 5-star boutique hotel has stunning contemporary interior design, a rooftop pool with panoramic city views and (on the same level) a restaurant for breakfast, light lunches, cocktails and dinner.

Lapa

As Janelas Verdes

Rua das Janelas Verdes 47; tel: 213-968 143; www.asjanelasverdes.com; tram 15; €€€

Next to the National Museum of Ancient Art, with views of the Tagus, this is a romantic little hotel occupying the 18th

The cosy library at As Janelas Verdes

century townhouse of one of Portugal's most famous writers, Eça de Queirós. In summer, breakfast is taken in the quiet, garden-like courtyard.

Lapa Palace

Rua do Pau de Bandeira 4; tel: 213-949 494; www.olissippohotels.com; tram 25 or bus 727; €€€€

This beautifully converted palatial mansion overlooks the River Tagus in the classy Lapa neighbourhood. Opened in 1992, it remains one of the city's most sumptuous and expensive hotels. It is surrounded by landscaped gardens and has an outdoor pool.

York House

Rua das Janelas Verdes 32; tel: 213-962 435; www.yorkhouselisboa.com; tram: 25 or bus 727; €€

Converted from a 17th-century Carmelite convent, this small hotel retains the feel of a serene retreat. It was opened as a guest house in 1880 by a couple of Yorkshire women (hence the name) and its English guests have included Graham Greene and John le Carré. Meals in summer are served in the plant-filled courtyard.

Belém

Altis Belém Hotel & Spa

Doca do Bom Sucesso; tel: 210-400 200; www.altishotels.com; tram 15; €€€€

Part of the Altis chain, this award-winning 5-star design hotel has wonderful views over the River Tagus in Belém. Enjoy gourmet cuisine in the Feitora restaurant (see page 66), riverside cocktails, a state-of-the-art spa and contemporary guest rooms.

Jerónimos 8

Rua dos Jerónimos 8; tel: 213-600 908; www.almeidahotels.pt; tram 15; €€

Go boutique in Belém at this stylish place, with sleek rooms that combine strong and neutral colours to harmonious effect. There are great views over the monastery. The hip red and white Bussaco Wine Bar serves rare Portuguese wines, simple dishes and delicious pastéis de Belém (custard tarts).

Parque das Nações

Myriad by Sana

Cais das Naus, Lote 2.21.01; tel: 211-107 600; www.myriad.pt; metro: Moscavide or Oriente; €€€€

At the northern end of the park and linked to the Vasco da Gama Tower, this sophisticated hotel is all light and water. It stands right on the wide estuary of the River Tagus – so wide it looks like the sea – and makes the most of the views of the Tagus and the Ponte Vasco da Gama. Decor is contemporary and stylish throughout. The 176 guest rooms come with Nespresso coffee machines, bathrobes and the option of a whirlpool bath or shower with massage jets.

Sintra

São Miguel Guest House

Rua Soto Maior 15, Sintra; tel: 219-244

Hotel Palácio Estoril has a storied history

088; www.saomiguelguesthouse.pt; €€
A gem of a guest house just down the road from the centre of Sintra. Teresa is a wonderfully welcoming hostess, and like the owner, Mafalda, is a font of knowledge on Sintra and beyond. Dating mainly from the 19th century, the house has period furnishings, elegant rooms and romantic views over the hills of Sintra. Breakfast is a treat, everything fresh and delicious, and weather permitting, is taken in the garden amid jacarandas, wisteria and roses.

Tivoli Palácio de Seteais

Rua Barbosa do Bocage 10, Sintra; tel: 219-233 222; www.tivolihotels.com; €€€€
A grand 5-star hotel within a beautiful 18th century palace with antiques, manicured gardens and superb views. Sports facilities include tennis courts, an outdoor pool and equestrian centre.

Cascais and Estoril

Hotel Palácio Estoril

Rua Particular, Estoril; tel: 214-648 000; www.palacioestorilhotel.com; €€€€
This 5-star hotel, established in 1930, is as palatial as the name suggests and during World War II, due to Portugal's neutrality, it became the haunt of many members of European royalty, as well as British and German spies. Today it offers modern comfort and amenities but retains the charm from a bygone era. Guests are entitled to special rates at its famous golf course.

Pergola House

Avenida Valbom 13, Cascais; tel: 214-840 040; www.pergolahouse.pt; €€
The 19th-century manor house has ten individually furnished rooms. All your needs are seen to: an excellent breakfast served in the flower-filled garden, or by the fireplace in winter, complimentary port served daily every afternoon, massage in your room on request. Anything else, just ask the staff. They are wonderfully helpful and friendly.

Arrábida Peninsula

Palmela

Pousada do Castelo de Palmela

Castelo de Palmela; tel: 212-351 226; www.pousadas.pt; €€
This hilltop hotel in a converted monastery has wonderful views of the Serra da Arrábida. It forms part of a medieval castle which was snatched from the Moors by King Afonso Henriques in the 12th century. Sink into a large comfy chair in the cloisters and dine on fine Portuguese fare in the former refectory.

Mafra

Quinta de Sant'Ana

Rua Direita 3, Mafra; tel: 261-963 550; www.quintadesantana.com; properties from €999 a week
Delightful wine estate half an hour from Lisbon and the beaches, providing self-catering accommodation with private or shared pools.

RESTAURANTS

Culinary hot spots have been popping up all over the city in recent years and there is now a huge diversity in the dining scene. An *ementa turística* is a fixed (not tourist) menu offered by many restaurants, particularly at lunchtime. It can be excellent value, typically including bread, soup, main course and dessert with a glass of wine, beer or soft drink included. Also worth trying is the *prato do dia* or dish of the day. When ordering wine you can't go too far wrong ordering the house wine *(vinho da casa)*. Ask the waiter for *tinto* (red), *branco* (white) or *vinho verde* (green wine).

Opening times are lunch *(almoço)* from noon until 3pm and dinner *(jantar)* from 7.30pm to at least 10pm, often much later. Locals tend to dine after 9pm so if you want the buzz, leave eating until later. Most restaurants close between lunch and dinner sittings but there are dozens of cafés and tea shops open all day for sandwiches or savoury and sweet pastries.

Castelo/Alfama

Pois Café

Rua de São João da Praça, 93-95; tel: 218-862 497; www.poiscafe.com; Mon noon–11pm, Tue–Sun 10am–11pm; tram 28 or 15; €

In a former spice warehouse, across the road from the cathedral, this Austrian-run café has a contemporary vibe: a fashionable mix of sofas and seats, modish young clientèle, books and newspapers and light, flavoursome dishes – as well as irresistible chocolate cheesecake served with a large dollop of cream.

Baixa/Cais do Sodré

Can the Can

Terreiro do Paço 82/83; tel: 218-851 392; www.canthecanlisboa.com; daily 9am–midnight; metro: Terreiro do Paço; €€

Tinned foods here are raised to gourmet levels. The Greek owner, Akis, is passionate about tinned fish, and serves the very best, maintaining that the fish goes straight into the can after the catch without losing any of the freshness. The chandelier is made of 3,000 tins!

Ibo

Arazém A Porta, Cais do Sodré; tel: 213-423 611; www.ibo-restaurante.pt; metro Tue–Sat lunch and dinner, Sun lunch only; metro: Cais do Sodré; €€€

In a former warehouse overlooking the Tagus, this stylishly-converted restaurant blends Portuguese and Mozam-

Price guide for a two-course meal for one with a glass of house wine:
€€€€ = over 40 euros
€€€ = 35–40 euros
€€ = 20–35 euros
€ = up to 20 euros

Time Out Mercado da Riberia is an unmissable attraction

bican flavours. Fish dishes include fried shrimps in filo pastry, fish and seafood curries, plainly grilled seabass and sole – and for carnivores, tenderloin steak.

Pap'Açorda

Mercado da Ribeira, Avenida 24 de Julho; tel: 213-464 811; www.papacorda.com; Tue–Sun noon–midnight, Thu–Sat until 2am; metro: Cais do Sodré; €€

This long-established restaurant in the Bairro Alto has moved to a stall in the Ribeira Market (see below), but the Portuguese fare is every bit as good as it was, and you can sample it 12–14 hours a day! Try the signature dish – the fabulous and filling açorda real (thick shellfish stew with lobster and shrimp), followed by the famous chocolate mousse.

Time Out Mercado da Ribeira

Avenida 24 de Julho 50; tel: 213-461 199; www.timeoutmarket.com; Sun to Wed 10am–midnight, Thur to Sat 10am–2am; metro: Cais do Sodré; €–€€

Occupying half of the old Mercado da Ribeira, Lisbon's market hall, this über-cool food market combines an affordable gourmet experience with a practical approach and a laid-back atmosphere. Since it opened in 2014, Lisboetas and tourists have been flocking here for both snacks and full meals. Go at any time of the day, select from the specialities of Portugal's top chefs, grab a glass of wine or fizz from a top supplier, find a space at one of the long wooden tables and enjoy.

Bairro Alto/Chiado/Principe Real

A Cevicheria

Rua Dom Pedro V 129, tel: 218-038 815; daily 12.30pm–midnight; metro: Restauradores; €€€

This tiny new fish restaurant is the talk of the town. You can't book tables, but at least while waiting (and it may be for 1–2 hours) you can enjoy a Pisco Sour and Peruvian popcorn at a pavement table. Expect fabulous flavours and combinations, beautifully presented dishes and a buzzing ambience. The pure *ceviche* is divine. The dominant decor is a giant octopus on the ceiling, crafted in sponge.

Alma

Rua Anchieta 15; tel: 213-470 650; www.almalisboa.pt; Tue–Sun lunch and dinner; metro: Baixa-Chiado; €€€€

Celebrity chef Henrique Sá Pessoa is well known for innovative Portuguese cuisine with a touch of the east. For a variety of his exquisite creations, splash out on the Alma menu (€80 per person) paired with the best of Portuguese wines.

By the Wine

Rua das Flores 41-43, Chiado; tel: 213-420 319; www.jmf.pt; daily 6pm–midnight; tram 28 or bus 202 or 758; €€

This is the flagship store of José Maria da Fonseca. Wines are served with a range of local delicacies such as Iberico ham, Azeitão cheese, salmon ceviche and oysters from the Sado Estuary.

Cervejaria da Trindade is a well-known beer hall

Cantinho do Avillez

Rua dos Duques de Bragança, 7; tel: 211-992 369; http://cantinhodoavillez.pt; daily lunch and dinner; tram 28 or metro: Baixa-Chiado; €€

This is the sister restaurant of José Avillez's two Michelin star Belcanto nearby (see page 48), offering the famous chef's dishes at more affordable prices. The ambience is informal and relaxed, with retro decor and friendly, professional service. Among Avillez's celebrated dishes are deep fried green beans with tartar sauce, cod with breadcrumbs, egg and 'exploding' olives, giant red shrimps with Thai flavours and Barrosã DOP hamburger with caramelised onion, *foie gras* and French fries.

De Castro

Rua Marcos Portugal, 1; tel: 215-903 077; www.decastro.pt; closed Mon and dinner on Sun; bus 773; €€

Renowned chef Miguel Castro e Silva heads this little restaurant in a pretty corner of the Principe Real district, with tables outside. The menu offers his classical dishes, such as clams with butter beans and codfish with spinach and sweet potato, as well as new innovative dishes and a good choice of tapas.

Cervejaria da Trindade

Rua Nova da Trindade 20; tel: 213-423 506; www.cervejariatrindade.pt; daily lunch and dinner; bus 202 or 758, tram 28; €€

This famous old beer hall and restaurant within a former monastery has spectacular panels of *azulejos* decorating the walls and serves popular Portuguese dishes and seafood specialities. Caters for large groups and has 100 seats outside.

100 Maneiras

Rua do Texeira 35; tel: 910-307 575; www.restaurante100maneiras.com; daily 7.30pm–2am; bus 202 or 758, Elevador da Glória; €€€€

This intimate, elegant restaurant in Bairro Alto is foodie heaven, offering a 10-course tasting menu (€55) where each dish is a surprise. Chef Ljobomir Stanisic, a Serbian native, also has a more informal, cheaper bistro at 9 Largo Trindade in Chiado.

Minibar

Rua António Maria Cardoso, 58; t el: 211-305 393; www.minibar.pt; daily 7pm–1am; metro: Baixa-Chiado; €€€€

This is the latest adventure of chef José Avillez – he now has five restaurants in the Chiado. Within the São Luiz Theatre, this evening-only venue is all about small gastronomical delicacies and finger food, created to surprise and entertain. A Ferrero Rocher chocolate, for example, will turn out to be *foie gras*.

Pão à Mesa Com Certeza

Rua Dom Pedro V, 44; tel: 966-122 675; Mon–Thu and Sun noon–1am, Fri and Sat noon–2am; bus 202 or 758; €€

Alfresco dining in the Bairro Alto

Bread *(pão)* is the theme of this new café/restaurant. Dishes such as fish stew or rustic soups are served in a hollowed-out loaf. Alternatively choose from fish dishes such as seared tuna with tempura, steaks or Portuguese sausage. Sandwiches are named after national personalities.

Sea Me

Rua do Loreto 21; tel: 213-461 564; www.peixariamoderna.com; daily lunch and dinner; metro: Baixa-Chiado, tram 28; €€€

Choose from a fish-market-like display of fresh seafood – or a lobster or crab from the tanks. There are sushi and sashimi options, salmon ceviche, seared tuna with wasabi ice cream, turbot, mullet, sole – and plenty more. Reservations recommended.

Sinal Vermelho

Rua das Gáveas, 89; tel: 213-461 252; closed Sun; bus 202 or 758; €€

In a side street of Bairro Alto, with tables spilling out on to the pavement, this friendly restaurant offers fish and pork specialities. As an appetiser, try clams Bulhão Pato (with garlic and coriander) or Bacalhau (dried salted cod) salad, followed perhaps by monkfish rice with shrimps and clams, fried little soles or grilled black pork loin.

Taberna Da Rua das Flores

Rua das Flores 103; tel: 213-479 418; Mon–Sat 11am–midnight; tram 28 or metro Baixa-Chiado; €€

Don't let the queues put you off this tiny, old-fashioned taverna. You can't reserve in advance but you can either arrive early (preferably before 7pm) or come later and queue with a drink or give your name and return later. Tapas include seafood, cerviche, goats cheese and historic Lisbon dishes such as *iscas* (pork liver), sweetbeads or *mexilhões à Bulhão Pato* (mussels with coriander, garlic and lemon). Leave room for the Portuguese almond cake called *Toucinho do Céu*, 'Bacon from Heaven', so-called because the recipe includes pork lard.

Tágide Wine & Tapas

Largo da Academia Nacional de Belas Artes 18; tel: 213-340 4010; www.restaurante tagide.com; closed Sun; metro: Baixa-Chiado or Tram 28; €

Enjoy excellent tapas, Portuguese wines and great city views in this elegant bar below the well known Tágide Restaurant. Typical tapas here include fried quail's egg and game chips, Iberian ham or clams with white wine and garlic.

Terra

Rua da Palmeira, 15 Príncipe Real; tel: 213-421 407; www.restauranteterra.pt; Tue–Sun lunch and dinner; bus 202 or 758; €

This is a favourite among vegetarians and vegans for its lavish buffet, with Mediterranean and Asian offerings, along with organic wines and home-made juices. The tree-shaded garden, with a fountain, is lit up in the evening.

Restaurants and bars in the former docks

Avenida and North Lisbon

Bon Jardim

Travessa Santo Antão 11; tel: 213-424 389; daily noon–11pm; metro: Restauradores; €

A good budget option, this simple place serves large helpings of chicken piri-piri (with chilli sauce) along with french fries and a simple salad. Speedy service.

Cervejaria Ramiro

Avenida Almirante Reis 1; tel: 218-851 024; closed Mon; 7 Aug to 6 Sep; www.cervejariaramiro.pt; metro: Intendente; €€€€

Long established, family-run beer house which offers some of the best fresh seafood in the city. It's all laid out for you: huge red shrimps, goose barnacles (*percebes*), grilled giant tiger prawns, oysters, clams and crabs. If you still have room, follow on with a *prego* (steak sandwich). No reservations so expect queues, but slick service once you're in.

O Talho

Rua Carlos Testa 1B; tel: 213-154 105; daily lunch and dinner; metro: São Sebastião; €€€

A carnivore's delight, combining a butcher's shop and restaurant. Award-winning chef Kiko looks for new ways to cook and taste meat in his 'laboratory kitchen'. One of the favourite dishes is beef tartare, prepared at the table.

Os Tibetanos

Rua do Salitre, 117; tel: 213-142 038; www.tibetanos.com; closed Sun; metro: Avenida; €

This was the first vegetarian restaurant to open in Lisbon. It offers Tibetan vegetarian pastries, seitan steak in mushroom sauce, crêpes with tofu and, as desserts, rose petal ice cream or the wickedly calorific Dolma tart, combining chestnuts and chocolate.

Vegetariano PSI

Alameda Santo António Capuchos; tel: 213-590 573; www.restaurante-psi.com; closed Sun; metro: Avenida; €

The chef trained at Le Cordon Bleu in Lima so expect plenty of different flavours and colours at this excellent vegetarian restaurant. Among the menu offerings are mango ceviche, beetroot humous, vegetarian curries and seitan kebabs. Attractive garden setting. No alcohol.

Estrela and south

Café de São Bento

Rua de São Bento 212; tel: 213-952 911; www.cafesaobento.com; closed lunch Sat and Sun; tram 28; €€

Next to the Palácio da Assembléia da República, home to Portugal's parliament, this restaurant opened over 30 years ago with the aim of recreating the Lisbon cafés of old, serving traditional *bife á marrare* (steak in a creamy pepper sauce). Its steaks have won many awards. Follow on with divine *tarte tatin*, served with ice cream.

Outstanding food, views and style at Fortaleza do Guincho

Mercado de Campo de Ourique

Rua Coelho da Rocha; www.mercadode campodeourique.pt; Sun–Wed 10am–11pm, Thur–Sat 10am–1am; tram 28; €–€€

The 1930s marketplace has been given a revamp and become a new, lively rendezvous for the city. Fruit, fish and veg stalls are now joined by an array of outlets where you can choose from take-away sushi and seafood, *petiscarias* (tapas), gourmet burgers or steak and chips, and sit at informal tables in the food hall. There is a good choice of Portuguese wines from the Copo d'Ourique wine bar – or for a G&T head for the 'Gin Corner'.

Solar dos Nunes

Rua dos Lusíadas 68-72, Alcântara; tel: 213-647 359; www.solardosnunes.com; closed Sun; bus 724, tram 15; €€

A delightful rustic restaurant specialising in Alentejo dishes such as *ameijoas à alentejano* (clam and pork casserole) and black pork loin with bread and garlic. Fish soup is a good bet, or you can select fish from the seafood tank. Fixed price lunch menu is available. Good value, and a great wine list.

Belém

À Margem

Doca Jardim do Bom Sucesso; tel: 917-824 149; www.amargem.com; summer: daily 10am–1am, off season closes 10pm Sun–Thur; tram 15; €

Trendy café in a converted shipping container by the riverside. Come for snacks, salads – or just a glass of wine while you watch the boats go by.

Sant'Apolónia

Bica do Sapato

Avenida Infante D. Henrique, Armazém B; tel: 218-810 320; www.bicadosapato. com; Mon 5pm–midnight, Tue–Sat noon–midnight, sushi bar: Mon–Sat 7.30pm–midnight; metro: Santa Apolónio; €€€

Fashionable riverside restaurant and a good spot for people-watching and boat-spotting. It's partly owned by John Malkovich and Catherine Deneuve, and is a popular haunt of celebrities and politicians. Choose from the cafeteria with river-view terrace, the more formal restaurant or the upstairs sushi bar. A popular brunch is served from Sept–June.

Cascais

Fortaleza do Guincho

Estrada do Guincho, tel: 214-870 491; www.fortalezadoguincho.pt; daily 12.30–3pm, 7.30–10.30pm; bus 405 and 415 from Cascais; €€€€

In 2016 Miguel Rocha Vieira took over as chef here – the first Portuguese to take the reins of this renowned, long-established restaurant. Expect the highest quality fish and seafood from Portuguese waters, outstanding wines and wonderful views of the Atlantic Ocean and Cabo da Roca. It's also a 5-star hotel and member of the Relais et Chateaux group.

NIGHTLIFE

Lisbon's nightlife is as diverse as you would expect of a capital city. You'll find trendy bars, late-night clubs, *fado* houses, dark *tabernas* and music to suit all tastes. For events and listings pick up the monthly Portuguese/English booklet, *Follow Me Lisboa*, free from tourist offices and some hotels. Remember to take cash with you – many venues don't accept credit cards. See also Entertainment on page 22 for information on the performing arts.

See also Entertainment on page 22 for information on the performing arts.

Rooftop bars

Park

Calçada do Combro, 58; tel: 215-914 011; Mon–Thur 1pm–3.30am, Sat 12.30pm–2am; tram: 28

A popular chill-out spot on the roof of a car park surrounded by greenery, with jazz, funk, soul and wonderful views of the Tagus. Also well known for its daily cultural and musical programme.

Sky Bar

Hotel Tivoli Lisboa, Avenida da Liberdade 185; tel: 213-198 900; www.tivolihotel.com; May–Oct 5pm–1am; metro: Avenida

Chill out on comfy sofas at this stylish bar on the top floor of the Tivoli Lisboa Hotel and enjoy music, fine dining and a dazzling vista of the city.

Terrace BA

Bairro Alto Hotel, Praça Luis de Camões 2, summer daily 10.30am–1am, winter Sun–Thur 10.30am–10pm, Fri–Sat 10.30am–1am; metro: Baixa-Chiado or tram 28

Perched on the top floor of the Bairro Alto Hotel, with amazing views over roofs and the river, particularly at sunset. A relaxed spot for a meal or candlelit drink.

Nightclubs and discos

Clube Ferroviário

Rua de Santa Apolónia 59; tel: 218-153 196; Mon–Wed 5pm–2am, Thu and Fri 5pm–4am, Sat noon–4am, Sun noon–midnight; metro: Santa Apolónia

Trendy train-themed restaurant, bar and disco in a former railworkers' club, with great views over the River Tagus from the terrace. Occasional theatre, open-air cinema and concerts.

Jamaica

Rua Nova do Carvalho 6-8; tel: 213-421 859; daily midnight–6am; metro: Cais do Sodré

A pioneer disco in the Cais do Sodré area, it vibrates to the sounds of reggae, soul and rock. Revellers head here when the Bairro Alto bars close and dance until dawn.

Lux

Avenida Infante Dom Henrique, Santa Apolónia; tel: 218-820 890; www.luxfragil.com; Thu–Sat 11pm–6am; metro: Santa Apolónia

The city's number one club, with top DJs, electronic music, varied concerts

Lux's lounge and discotheque

and river-view roof terrace. The converted docklands warehouse is partly owned by actor John Malkovich. If you arrive after 2am or don't look the part, you may be turned away.

Bars

Chapitô
Costa do Castelo 7; tel: 218-855 550; daily 10pm–2am; winter Tue–Sun 10pm–2am; bus: 73

Take in jaw-dropping city views over a sundowner at this bar near the castle. Tapas and hearty Portuguese fare are also on offer. Chapitô is a non profit-making organisation for training through performing arts, and the complex includes a theatre and circus school.

Cinco Lounge
Rua Ruben António Leitão; tel: 213 424 033; www.cincolounge.com; daily 9pm–2am; metro: Rato or bus 773

Seductive and sophisticated British-owned bar with great cocktails, made of fresh fruit and spices, with and without alcohol. Unusually, the music has decibel levels that enable conversation.

Casas de Fado

Prices for food are noticeably higher than restaurants (typically €50 per person) but that of course includes the show. There is often a minimum charge until 10–11pm, typically €25/35, which goes towards your meal, then later it's €10–18. See also Parreirinha de Alfama and O Faia, Route 3.

Café Luso
Travessa da Queimada 10; tel: 213-422 281; www.cafeluso.pt; daily 7.30pm–2am; tram 28, bus 758

The atmospheric Café Luso has hosted *fado* and folk dances since 1827, making it the oldest *fado* house in Bairro Alto. Artists sing from 10pm–2am and food is available.

Tasca do Chico
Rua do Diário de Noticias 39; tel: 965-059 670; daily 7pm–2am; tram 28, bus 758

This small, sought-after, dimly-lit bar puts on *fado vadio* (laid-back *fado* where anyone can get up and sing) on Monday and Wednesday evenings. Bar tapas are on offer.

Casinos

Casino Estoril
Avenida Dr Stanley Ho, Estoril; tel: 214-667 700; daily 3pm–3am; www.casino-estoril. pt (in Portuguese only); trains from Cais do Sodré

The largest casino in Europe, this is a big draw for gamblers and was the inspiration for Ian Fleming's *Casino Royale*. Passports are required. Shows are also staged here and there is a choice of restaurants including the excellent Chinese Mandarim restaurant. Since 2006 the casino has seen competition from the Casino Lisboa at the Parque das Nações (www.casinolisboa.pt) which has 700 slot machines, 22 gaming tables, restaurants, bars and also a large auditorium.

Clasic azulejos

A–Z

A

Age restrictions

The age of consent in Portugal is 14. It is an offence to supply or sell alcoholic drinks to those under 18. The minimum age for driving is 17, but to hire a car you must be 18 or older, depending on the car-hire company.

B

Budgeting

Accommodation

A double room in a simple hotel is €60–100, in the mid-range category from €100–150 and for a 4-star plus, expect to pay over €200. Most prices do not include breakfast. Rates fluctuate according to the season and are usually at their highest from May to September and lowest in January and February.

Drinks and meals

A coffee costs anything from 70 cents (espresso in a local bar) to €2.80 (cappuccino served in a smart bar on a main square); beer is €1.50–2.50. Most restaurants offer a midday meal bargain, called an *ementa* turística, often no more than €10–15 for a fixed-price, three-course meal. A three-course meal with wine in a mid-range restaurant would be around €30, or in an upmarket restaurant from €40 upwards.

Museums

Admission fees range from €2.50–10. Some museums are free on the first Sunday of the month, others every Sunday but mornings only. Considerable concessions are offered to those over 65 and students (ID often required); very young children are usually free.

Transport

A taxi from the airport to the city centre costs €15–20. A single bus ticket costs €1.80 on buses, €2.85 on trams, and is reduced to €1.40 if charged on a pre-paid Viva Viagem card (€0.50), which can be purchased from metro stations and ticket machines. You can charge it for a 24-hour session, which costs €6 and is valid for unlimited journeys on the Carris network (the latter includes metro, buses, trams and funiculars such as the Elevador de Sant Justa). If you're travelling around the city for more than a day, your best bet is a reloadable Viva Viagem card, which can be loaded up to €20. Lisbon's tourist offices offer a discount Lisboa Card that entitles holders to free metro, bus, tram and lift transport, free entry into 27 museums and monuments (including sights outside Lisbon), and discounts on tourist attractions such as city tours and some shops. The card

is available for 24, 48 or 72 hours at €18.50, €31.50 and €39 respectively, with substantial reductions for children.

C

Children

With its vintage trams, funiculars, elevators and ferries and river trips, Lisbon offers some great ways to entertain children just by touring around the city. Catch the cheap ferry to Cacilhas across the river, and take the 101 bus to the Cristo Rei statue with a lift up to the viewing platform, or a bus from Cacilhas to the beaches of Costa da Caparica.

The indisputable number one Lisbon attraction for children is the **Oceanarium** at the Parque das Nações (see page 68), which is one of the biggest in the world. The park also has playgrounds, fountains, aerial cable cars and a hands-on science museum. The **Jardim Zoológico** (Zoo, Estrada be Benfica 158-160; www.zoo.pt; daily Apr–late Sep 10am–8pm, off season 10am–6pm, last admission 1hr 15 mins before closing time; metro: Jardim Zoológico) has 2,000 animals, plus a cable car and miniature train. Shows include dolphin displays and feeding of pelicans and sea lions. The **Museu da Marioneta** (Puppet Museum, see page 57) has puppets from all over the world and stages shows. In Belém, the **Planetário Calouste Gulbenkian** has weekend planetarium sessions: Saturday 3pm and 6pm, Sunday 11.30am, 3pm and 4pm. For children the most entertaining of the city tours is the amphibious HIPPOtrip (www.hippotrip.com), which runs every two hours, tours the centre, then plunges into the river.

Children under four travel free of charge on public transport; those between 4 and 12 pay half-price.

Clothing

Take comfy walking shoes for the steep hills and uneven cobbled streets. Spring and autumn are relatively balmy so you won't need anything heavier than a sweater in the daytime and light jacket at night. Summer days can be very hot but pack a wrap or sweater for cooler, windy evenings. Winters are mild but you will need warmer clothes and rainwear.

Crime and safety

Lisbon traditionally has been one of Europe's more laid-back and safe cities, but with the influx of tourists pick-pocketing is on the rise. Leave valuables in the hotel safe and keep an eye on handbags, mobile phones and wallets. Be particularly alert on public transport (especially Tram 28), in cafés on Rossio, the Alfama area, markets and other tourist hotspots. Report theft to your hotel, nearest police station or local tourist office. The police emergency number is 112. At night, take care around the narrow dark streets of the Mouraria, Alfama and Graça. Always lock cars and never leave anything of value in view.

A marching band for an Easter parade

Customs

Free exchange of non-duty-free goods for personal use is allowed between countries within the EU. Those from non-EU countries should refer to their home country's regulating organisation for a current list of import restrictions. If you are a non-EU resident you may be able to reclaim VAT on some items bought within Portugal.

D

Disabled travellers

Lisbon's cobbled streets and steep hills don't make it easy for disabled travellers and although facilities have greatly improved, it is not an ideal destination for the disabled. Areas such as Belém, parts of Baixa and Parque das Nações (the most accessible of all) are easier to get around, as they are flat with broad streets and pavements. Only 36 out of 56 metro stations have full facilities (see www.metrolisboa.pt for details). Vintage trams are overcrowded and very tricky for wheelchairs, and many of the modern tram stops have steps. Carris (www.carris.pt) offer a bus service for those with reduced mobility, for which you will need to book ahead. Some buses have access ramps and spaces for wheelchairs. Taxis are often the best option – especially to the castle. Taxi drivers tend to be helpful and friendly and the prices are low. Accessible Portugal (www.accessibleportugal.com) offer holidays for the disabled.

E

Electricity

The electrical current in Portugal is 220V; AC and sockets take two-pin, round-pronged plugs. For US appliances, 220v transformers and plug adaptors are required.

Embassies

Australia (Embassy): Avenida da Liberdade 200, Lisbon, tel: 213-101 500; www.portugal.embassy.gov.au.

Canada (Embassy): Avenida da Liberdade 198-200, 3rd floor, Lisbon; tel: 213 164 600; www.canadainternational.gc.ca/portugal

UK (Embassy): Rua de São Bernardo 33, tel: 213-924 000; www.gov.uk/government/world/portugal.

US: Avenida das Forças Armadas, 16, Lisbon; tel: 217-273 300; https://portugal.usembassy.gov.

Emergencies

Police, Fire and Ambulance: 112
Tourist Police: 213-421 634 and 213-421 623.

Etiquette

Lisboetas take care over their attire and tend to dress fashionably but rarely very formally. Virtually no establishments require a tie.

It is respectful not to flash flesh (cover arms and legs) when visiting churches.

Flowers for sale on Rua Augusta

F

Festivals and events

The following are just some of the main traditional festivals but the Portuguese love an excuse for a party so expect myriad smaller events. Check out details with tourist information offices.

February–March: Carnival – Processions and fireworks

March: Moda Lisboa – Lisbon fashion week

March–April: Peixe em Lisboa – Fish festival. Dias da Música em Belém – music festival at the Centro Cultural, Belém.

May: IndieLisboa – Portugal's biggest independent film festival

May–June: Alkantara Art Festival. Rock in Rio (in even years) – five-day rock festival, featuring international stars. Sintra music festival.

June: Festas dos Santos Populares – including Festival of St Anthony, patron saint of Lisbon. Faz Música Lisboa – live music including Blues, *fado*, jazz and rock in eight city venues.

July: Nos Alive – an open-air rock, indie and pop festival (www.optimusalive.com). Superbock Superrock – mega rock festival. Sintra music festival.

August: Jazz em Agosto – jazz concerts at the Gulbenkian open-air amphitheatre. Cascais Festas do Mar (Sea Festival) – 10 days of music from pop and rock to *fado*. Estoril International Music Festival.

October: Estoril Open Golf Tournament.

November: Arte Lisboa – contemporary art fair. Lisbon and Estoril Film Festival.

G

Gay and lesbian travellers

Lisbon is the most important city in Portugal's gay scene, offering plenty of bars and clubs catering for a gay crowd. The scene centres around late night gay bars in the Praça do Príncipe Real quarter, and also in nearby Bairro Alto. Out of Lisbon, at the south end of the Costa da Caparica, beach No 19 on the narrow-gauge railway is a very popular hangout.

A good queer travel website is www.patroc.com/lisbon, with information on hotels, bars, clubs, parties and events. Another useful site is www.portugal-gay.pt, on gay life throughout Portugal. The Centro LGBT (Rua dos Fanqueiros 40, Baixa, tel: 218-873 918; www.ilga-portugal.pt [website in Portuguese only]) provides information and advice.

H

Hours and holidays

Opening hours

Banks: Mon–Fri 8.30am–3pm

Museums and galleries: the main closing day in Lisbon is Monday, otherwise most museums open all day.

Restaurants: lunch noon–3pm, dinner 7–10pm or later. Many close for one day a week, often Sunday or Monday. Some restaurants close for part or the whole of August.

War memorial, Belém

Shops: Mon–Sat 9.30/10am–7pm though some shut at 1pm on Saturday and some of the smaller shops close for lunch. Shopping centres have very long hours, typically daily 10am to midnight, including Sunday.

Public holidays

Banks, offices and many shops and museums close on public holidays.

1 January Ano Novo (New Year's day)
25 April Dia da Liberdade (1974 Revolution DayM
1 May Dia do Trabalhador (Labour Day)
10 June Dia de Camões (Camões's Day), also known as Portugal Day
15 August Assunção (Assumption)
5 October Implantação da República (Republic Day)
1 November Todos-os-Santos (All Saints' Day)
8 December Imaculada Conceição (Immaculate Conception)
25 December Natal (Christmas Day)

Moveable dates: Carnaval (Carnival/Shrove Tuesday), Sexta-feira Santa (Good Friday) and Corpo de Deus (Corpus Christi), 9th Thursday after Easter.

Lisbon, Estoril and Cascais have a local holiday on 13 June in honour of St Anthony (Santo António).

Internet

Lisbon has plenty of internet cafés (ask at tourist offices for details) and almost all hotels have Wi-Fi throughout. While it is free in cheaper hotels there may be a charge in high-end accommodation.

L

Language

Many Portuguese speak English in Lisbon, especially in the tourist trade (see page 134).

M

Media

Print media

British newspapers usually turn up on the same day as publication. The weekly *Portugal News*, (www.theportugalnews.com) published in the Algarve, is the country's main English-language paper and covers news and stories from around the country.

Useful free Portuguese/English booklets include the monthly **Follow Me Lisboa**, packed with listings and other information and **Lisboa Convida** in print and online (www.lisboa.convida.pt), a six-monthly shopping and leisure guide. They are available from tourist offices and some hotels.

TV and radio

Four television channels are widely available in Portugal, two of them state-run, RTP1 and RTP2, and two privately-owned, SIC and TVI. Foreign films are usually show in the original language with subtitles. Most hotels have English-language channels such as BBC News and CNN.

Fishing boats, Costa da Caparica

Money

Currency

The euro (€) is the official currency used in Portugal. Notes are denominated in 5, 10, 20, 50, 100, 200 and 500 euros; coins in 1 and 2 euros and 1, 2, 5, 10, 20 and 50 cents.

Credit cards

MasterCard and Visa are the most widely accepted credit cards. Many places don't accept American Express. Some small shops and restaurants take cash only; you also need to have cash handy for museums.

Cash machines

ATMs are widespread. You can take out a maximum of €200 a day.

Tipping and taxes

In most restaurants service is included, but if you are pleased with the service leave up to 5 percent; if service is not included, 10 percent. Taxi drivers won't necessarily expect a tip but you can always round up the fare or give an extra euro.

P

Post

Lisbon's main post office is at Praça dos Restauradores, 58 (opposite the tourist office, Mon–Fri 8am–8pm, Sat 9am–6pm). Local post offices are open Mon–Fri 9am–6pm; main branch offices also operate on Saturday until noon. You can purchase stamps from some tobacconists and kiosks, as well as at post offices.

R

Religion

The Portuguese are predominantly Roman Catholic, a fact reflected in surviving religious rituals and saints' days that are public holidays. A service is held in English at 11.30am on Sunday at St George's (Anglican) Church in Estrela, at Rua São Jorge (www.lisbon anglicans.org).

S

Smoking

Smoking is still quite common in Portugal and a few restaurants have their own special smoking section. Otherwise smokers sit outside on the terrace. Smoking is banned on public transport and museums.

T

Telephones

Portugal's country code is **351**. The local area code – **21** in the case of Lisbon and the Estoril Coast, including Sintra – must be dialled before all phone numbers, including local calls. To make an international call, dial 00 followed by the country code (UK 44, US 1, Australia 61, Canada and the US 1) plus

Beach hut at Praia da Saúde

the phone number including the area code, but without the initial 'O' where there is one. Public telephones are not as plentiful as they used to be and most of them take phonecards, which have to be purchased from post offices, newsagents and telephone offices

To save on roaming charges you can buy an affordable local SIM card from one of the mobile network operators.

Time zones

Portugal maintains Greenwich Mean Time (GMT), along with the UK, and is therefore one hour behind the rest of the EU. From the last Sunday in March until the last Sun in October, the clocks are moved one hour ahead for summer time, GMT + 1. If it is noon in Lisbon it will be 7am in New York, 1pm in Paris and 9pm in Sydney.

Toilets

Public toilets can be hard to find but you can always use a bar or café. Normally toilets are marked H for *Homens*, (men's) or S for *Senhoras* (women's)

Tourist information

Lisbon has 14 *Ask Me Lisboa* information points where you can buy the Lisboa Card (see Budgeting), book accommodation and pick up tourist information. The following are the main information points:
Arrivals Hall, Lisbon airport; tel: 218-450 660; daily 7am–midnight
Palácio Foz, Praça dos Restauradores; tel: 213-463 314; daily 9am–8pm

Praça do Comércio 78-81; tel: 910-517 886; daily 10am–8pm; and across the square a second Ask Me Lisboa office; tel: 210-312 810; 9am–8pm
Opposite the monastery in Belém; tel: 213-658 435; Tue–Sat 10am–1pm, 2–6pm;

Outside Lisbon

Sintra: Praça da República 23 (in the town centre); tel: 211-932 545; daily 9.30am–6pm. There is also an office at the station.
Cascais: Largo Cidade Vitória; tel: 912-034 214; daily 9am–6pm, summer until 8pm.

Tours and cruises

Some of the finest views of Lisbon are seen from the River Tagus. From April–October, Transtejo (www.transtejo.pt) offer boat trips, departing from Terreiro do Paço ferry terminal in the city centre. A single 24-hour ticket enables you to hop-on and hop-off on both banks (it also includes buses and trams).

More expensive but very special are the two-hour, all-year sailing cruises, organised by Tagus Cruises (www.taguscruises.com; tel: 925 610 034; minimum two people). Yachts set sail from Doca do Bom Sucesso close to Belém tower. The boat floats past riverside landmarks, affording fine views of Cristo Rei, Ponte 25 de Abril, the Torre de Belém and other monuments as far as Alfama. Best of all are the sunset tours, where you sit back with a glass of

Selling vegetables in the Mercado da Ribeira

wine as you watch the sun sink below the suspension bridge.

Transport

Getting to Lisbon

Arrival by air

Lisbon's airport is linked by scheduled daily non-stop flights from several European cities and from the east coast of the United States. Flights from Canada, Australia and New Zealand go through London or another European capital. TAP/Air Portugal (www.flytap.com) is Portugal's national airline and has wide international links, including from the US. There are regular TAP flights to Lisbon from London Gatwick and Heathrow. British Airways (www.ba.com) operate scheduled services from London Heathrow. Budget airlines offering services from the UK direct to Lisbon include easyJet (www.easyjet.com) from Gatwick, Luton, Liverpool, Bristol and Edinburgh; Ryanair (www.ryanair.com) from London Stansted and Manchester and Monarch (www.monarch.co.uk) from Birmingham, Manchester and Gatwick. From Ireland, direct flights operate from Dublin with Aer Lingus and Ryanair.

Lisbon Airport (www.aeroportolisboa.pt) is just 5 miles (8km) northeast of the city and is well served by metro, bus and taxi. The airport is the terminus of the metro's red line. Trains operate from 6.30am–1am, but you will have to change at Alameda for the city centre. The shuttle AeroBus (www.aerobus.pt),

Line 1, links the airport to main points of the city centre (8am–11pm, every 20–25 mins, one way €3.50, child 4–10 €2) and takes around half an hour. The ticket also gives you unlimited access to the bus network for the rest of the day.

Arrival by sea and rail

Lisbon is a major port and several cruise ships include a call in the capital. Portugal is linked to the European railway network and connections to Lisbon are possible from points throughout Spain, France and the rest of mainland Europe.

Buses and trams

The bus and tram network, operated by Carris (www.cmt.pt), covers virtually the whole city. Rush hour is notoriously busy so expect long waits. The Carris website has detailed information on routes, schedules and maps. Buses are yellow and usually operate between 6.30am and midnight. A *paragem* is a bus stop. For tickets see Budgeting. Tickets must be validated in the machine on the bus or tram.

There are two types of trams, the charming vintage models and the new longer ones with sleek interiors. Trams operate in a limited area of the city. The most popular (and crowded) tourist tram is the No 28 (see Route 9) which runs via Estrela, Bairro Alto/Chiado, Baixa and the castle. Most trams are entered at the front, where you can buy a ticket from the driver or validate your pre-paid ticket.

In the arcades flanking Praça do Comércio

Funiculars and lifts

Funiculars and lifts can save legwork on the city's hills. They are included in a one day transport pass or Viva Viagem card, otherwise they are expensive for what is a very short ride.

Metro

Lisbon's underground Metropolitano (www.metrolisboa.pt) has four colour-coded lines (red, green, yellow and blue) and is easy to use. The service operates from 6.30am–1am. The red line links the city to the airport. Certain stations link up with the railway stations and ferry termini. The cheapest way to travel is to buy an electronic *Viva Viagem* card, available at metro vending machines and ticket offices, which you then charge up as you go (see Budgeting).

Trains (Comboios)

Lisbon has four railway stations: The main ones for national and international travel are Santa Apolónia and Estação do Oriente. Commuter trains for the western suburbs, Estoril and Cascais, depart from Cais do Sodré about every 20 minutes, and take 30 minutes, while trains for Sintra depart from Rossio station, also every 20 minutes (journey time 40 minutes). The national rail company is CP (Comboios de Portugal) which connects the capital to the major cities of the country.

Taxis

Taxis are cheap by European standards. Most are black and green. Taxi ranks can be found at main squares and stations, but can also be hailed in the street. The fare is shown on the meter – check that it's running before you set off. There are extra charges from 9pm–6am and at weekends, and for luggage placed in the boot. To order a taxi: Teletáxis: 218-111 111; Autocoope: 217-932 756.

Ferries

The two main ferry stations for the River Tagus's southern shore are Estação Fluvial Terreiro do Paço for Barreiro and Cais do Sodré for Cacilhas, Montijo and Seixal.

By bike

Given Lisbon's hilly terrain, uneven streets and traffic-filled lanes, few tourists choose to hire a bike, or if they do it's an electric one. The areas you might consider on a conventional bike is the riverside track which goes from Cais do Sodré to Belém (and Belém itself, which is very flat), and Parque das Nações, where bikes can be hired. Lisbon Cycle Tours (www.lisboncycletours.com) do an excellent, three-hour seven-hills tour on electric bikes showing you parts of the city most tourists don't penetrate.

Car hire

Major international firms such as Avis, Hertz, Europcar and Budget have desks at the airport and locations in Lisbon, but for the best deals book online in advance. The minimum age of hiring a car is 21–25 (depending on the company) and anyone hiring must have held a valid licence for

A tourist sightseeing bus

at least one year. Rental companies will accept your home country's national driving license, but you must show your passport. Third-party insurance should be included in the basic charge. All car rental contracts in Portugal have excess amounts of around €1,000. The cost to waive the excess is around €15 a day; it is far cheaper to take out an excess insurance policy in advance.

Driving

Try to avoid driving in Lisbon. Roads are narrow and frequently congested, signage is almost non-existent, as is parking in the historic centre. For most visitors, public transport and the inexpensive private taxis are vastly superior methods of navigating the city. There is also an excellent train service to Cascais and Sintra, and buses to Óbidos, Mafra and Sesimbra. However, a car is very useful for exploring the Alentejo region or the Serra da Arrábida national park.

To bring your own car into Portugal you will need your national driving licence, registration papers and insurance. The main roads of Portugal are generally in good repair.

Rules and regulations

The rules of the road are the same as in most western European countries. Drive on the right. The vehicle already on the roundabout has priority unless road markings or lights indicate otherwise. Seat belts are compulsory and a heavy fine can be imposed for not wearing one.

Speed limits are 120km/h (75mph) on motorways, 100km (62.5mph) on roads restricted to motor vehicles, 90km/h (56mph) on other roads and 50km/h (37mph) in urban areas.

V

Visas and passports

For EU citizens, a valid passport or identity card is all that is need to enter Portugal for stays of up to 90 days. Citizens of Australia, Canada, New Zealand and the US require only a valid passport. For stays of more than 90 days, a visa or residence permit is required.

W

Websites

www.visitlisboa.com – official tourist office site
www.askmelisboa.com – official tourist office site
www.visitportugal.com – official tourism site for Portugal
www.cmt.pt – public transport website
www.cp.pt – Caminhos de Portugal, the railway network
www.lisbonlux.com – a useful guide to the city

Women

Lisbon is fairly safe but it is best to avoid walking alone in deserted areas at night. Women should also keep an eye on handbags and jewellery in Bairro Alto, Cais do Sodré and Alfama.

Azulejo signage

LANGUAGE

Portuguese is the sixth most spoken language in the world with around 220 million native speakers and 260 million total speakers. Any school Spanish may help with signs and menus, but will not unlock the mysteries of spoken Portuguese, with its many nasal sounds. Almost all hotels have staff who speak English and unless you go off the beaten track you should have little problem communicating in most shops or restaurants. Almost everyone understands Spanish and many speak French, but just learning a few simple words and phrases in Portuguese will certainly enhance your visit and help if you are off the tourist circuit. Here are a few basics to help you get started.

General

hello (good morning) *bom dia*
good afternoon/evening *boa tarde*
good night *boa noite*
goodbye *adeus*
yes *sim*
no *não*
thank you *obrigado (masc) obrigada (fem)*
many thanks *muito obrigado*
you're welcome *de nada*
please *faz favor, por favor*
I need... *preciso...*
I'm sorry *desculpe-me*
excuse me *com licença*

I don't know *não sei*
I don't understand *não comprendo*
do you speak English? French *fala inglês? francês?*
please speak slowly *faz favor de falar devagar*
please say that again *diga outra vez, se faz favor*
how much does it cost? *quanto custa?*

At a bar/restaurant

have you got a table for....... *tem uma mesa para?*
may we have the menu? *a ementa se faz favor*
what do you recommend? *que recomenda?*
fixed-price menu *a ementa turística*
what wine do you recommend? *qual é o vinho que recomenda?*
mineral water (still) *agua sem gás; (fizzy) agua com gás*
red (mature)/white wine ("green") *vinho tinto (maduro)/branco (verde)*
bottle/half bottle *garrafa/meia garrafa*
beer *cerveja*
cheers! *saúde!*
do you take credit cards? *aceitam cartões de credito?*
the bill please *a conta se faz favor*
toilets (ladies/gents, men/women) *casa de banho (senhoras/senhores, homens/mulheres)*

Newspapers for sale

Numbers

1 *um/uma*
2 *dois/duas*
3 *três*
4 *quatro*
5 *cinco*
6 *seis*
7 *sete*
8 *oito*
9 *nove*
10 *dez*
20 *vinte*
30 *trinta*
40 *quarenta*
50 *cinquenta*
100 *cem*
1,000 *mil*

Getting around

how do I get to…? *como se vai para…?*
where is…? *onde é…?*
left/right *esquerda/direita*
straight on *sempre em frente*
what time do you open/close? *a que hora abre/fecha?*
can you help me? *pode ajudar-me?*
can you show me? *pode mostrar me?*
I'm lost *estou perdido/a*
can we walk there? *podemos ir a pé?*
railway station *estação de comboio*
bus station *estação de autocarros*
train *comboio*
return ticket *bilhete de ida e volta*
single ticket *bilhete de ida*
ticket office *bilheteria*

Days of the week

Sunday *domingo*
Monday *segunda-feira*
Tuesday *terça-feira*
Wednesday *quarta-feira*
Thursday *quinta-feira*
Friday *sexta-feira*
Saturday *sábado*
Today *hoje*
Yesterday *ontem*
Tomorrow *amanhã*

Online

Where is an internet café? *Onde fica um Internet café?*
Can I access the internet here? *Tenho acesso à internet aqui?*
What is the WiFi password? *Qual é a senha do WiFi?*
Is the WiFi free? *O WiFi é grátis?*
How do I log on/log off? *Como faço o logon/logoff?*
Can I..? *Posso..?*
What's your email? *Qual é o seu e-mail?*
My email is…. *O meu e-mail é.....*
To print *imprimir*

Social media

Are you on Facebook/Twitter? *Esta no Facebook/Twitter?*
What's your user name? *Qual é o seu nome de utilizador?*
I'll add you as a friend *Vou adicioná-lo como amigo*
I'll follow you on Twitter *Vou segui-lo no Twitter*
I'll put the pictures on Facebook/Instagram *Vou colocar as fotos no Facebook/Instagram*

An azulejo illustration of 'The Lusiads'

BOOKS AND FILM

A good number of books on Portugal are available in English, and the list below is just a tiny selection.

Lisbon has attracted foreign writers for several centuries. In 1754 Henry Fielding, author of *Tom Jones*, came here for his health but died two months' later (he is buried in the city's English cemetery). By the end of the 18th century, grand tours were beginning to attract romantic imaginations. The most famous visitors included William Beckford, who lived near Sintra, and Byron, Southey and Keats, who were all also inspired by Sintra. Byron was not always complimentary about Portugal. In his epic poem, *Childe Harold*, the Portuguese – described as 'Lusian brute' – are picked out for special attack.

George Borrow, the intrepid 19th century author and Bible salesman who travelled to Portugal in 1835, has left to posterity some wonderfully descriptive accounts of his journeys. He waxed lyrical about Lisbon which he thought 'as much deserving the attention of the artist as even Rome itself'.

Portuguese writers

Luís de Camões Portugal's great national poet, author of the great epic poem, *The Lusiads*, written in 1572 and describing Vasco da Gama's discovery of the sea route to India.

Eça de Queirós (1845–1900) is Por-

tugal's leading realist writer of the 19th century, often ranked alongside Balzac and Dickens. His most popular work is *The Maias*, about a wealthy family in fin-de-siècle Lisbon.

Eugénio Lisboa has edited a number of books of poetry and short stories, including *The Anarchist Banker and Other Portuguese Stories*, and *Professor Pfiglzz and His Strange Companion*.

Fernando Pessoa (1888–1935) is second only to Camões in the list of illustrious Portuguese poets. He wrote under other names: Alberto Caeiro, Ricardo Reis and Álvaro de Campos, transforming his style with each. His *Book of Disquiet* contains his disturbing meditations around Chiado.

José Saramago (1922–2010) received the Nobel Prize for Literature in 1998, hastening the translation of his works into English. *Journey to Portugal: In Pursuit of Portugal's History and Culture* is a good place to start, a wonderful travelogue full of detailed insight.

Miguel Torga's autobiography, *The Creation of the World* recalls his Trás-os-Montes childhood in northern Portugal, his boyhood in Brazil and the return to his native village to work as a doctor.

Books about Portugal

Non-fiction

A Concise History of Portugal by David

A shot from 'Night Train To Lisbon'

Birmingham. A standard, with many illustrations.

Backwards Out of the Big World: A Voyage into Portugal by Paul Hyland. Following in the steps of Henry Fielding from Lisbon to the Spanish border.

The First Global Village: How Portugal Changed the World, by Martin Page (updated 2015). A comprehensive and very readable history by a journalist with a deep knowledge of the city and its people.

The Last Day: Wrath, Ruin and Reason in the Great Lisbon Earthquake of 1755 by Nicholas Shrady. Riveting history of the earthquake and the shock waves it sent throughout western civilisation.

Portuguese Voyages 1498-1663: edited by Charles David Ley. Tales from the Great Age of Discovery, drawn from contemporary accounts.

Republican Portugal, a Political History 1910-1926 by Douglas L. Wheeler. A fascinating account of the period between monarchy and dictatorship when Portugal endured 45 successive governments.

They Went to Portugal by Rose Macaulay. A lively account of Lisbon's visitors, mainly British, from the Crusaders to the romantic writers of the 19th century.

Fiction

The Last Kabbalist of Lisbon by Richard Zimler. Historical thriller set in Lisbon in 1506, when 'New Christian' Jewish converts were being murdered.

The Migrant Painter of Birds by Lidia Jorge. A beautifully crafted poetic novel by the feminist novelist about a girl from a Portuguese farming family and her absent father.

A Small Death in Lisbon by Robert Wilson. Compelling award-winning thriller with plots intertwining between Portugal in World War II and the 1990s.

Films

The Lovers of Lisbon (1955) French film based on the novel Les Amants du Tage. Two French exiles in Lisbon who have both murdered their spouses fall in love.

Lisbon (1956) A US adventure romance, where an American smuggler is hired to rescue a wealthy industrialist who is a prisoner behind the Iron Curtain. Beautifully shot and worth watching for the sumptuous scenes of Lisbon alone.

Pereira Declares (1996) The political awakening of a cautious journalist, Dr Pereira (played by Marcello Mastroianni) during the Salazar dictatorship. Based on the eponymous book by Antonio Tabucchi.

Night Train to Lisbon (2013) directed by Bille August and starring Jeremy Irons, the film is based on the European best-selling novel, Night Train to Lisbon, by Pascar Mercier.

Haircut (2014) directed by Joaquim Sapinho. Independent postmodern Portuguese film, examining crisis and compromise in the relationship of a young couple in the 1990s. The film is shot in well-known locations around Lisbon.

For cinematic tours of Lisbon, available in English: www.lisbonmovietour.com.

ABOUT THIS BOOK

This *Explore Guide* has been produced by the editors of Insight Guides, whose books have set the standard for visual travel guides since 1970. With top-quality photography and authoritative recommendations, these guidebooks bring you the very best routes and itineraries in the world's most exciting destinations.

BEST ROUTES

The routes in the book provide something to suit all budgets, tastes and trip lengths. As well as covering the destination's many classic attractions, the itineraries track lesser-known sights, and there are also excursions for those who want to extend their visit outside the city. The routes embrace a range of interests, so whether you are an art fan, a gourmet, a history buff or have kids to entertain, you will find an option to suit.

We recommend reading the whole of a route before setting out. This should help you to familiarise yourself with it and enable you to plan where to stop for refreshments – options are shown in the 'Food and Drink' box at the end of each tour.

For our pick of the tours by theme, consult Recommended Routes for... (see pages 6–7).

INTRODUCTION

The routes are set in context by this introductory section, giving an overview of the destination to set the scene, plus background information on food and drink, shopping and more, while a succinct history timeline highlights the key events over the centuries.

DIRECTORY

Also supporting the routes is a Directory chapter, with a clearly organised A–Z of practical information, our pick of where to stay while you are there and select restaurant listings; these eateries complement the more low-key cafés and restaurants that feature within the routes and are intended to offer a wider choice for evening dining. Also included here are some nightlife listings, plus a handy language guide and our recommendations for books and films about the destination.

ABOUT THE AUTHOR

Susie Boulton fell in love with Portugal as a child, assisting her grandmother on a water divining mission in the Algarve before the tidal wave of tourism. She wrote her first guidebook to Lisbon in 1992 and has seen the city change from what felt like a relatively remote outpost to one of the most exciting capitals in Europe. As a freelance travel writer, Susie has written around 30 guidebooks to European destinations, including many titles for Insight Guides and Berlitz.

CONTACT THE EDITORS

We hope you find this Explore Guide useful, interesting and a pleasure to read. If you have any questions or feedback on the text, pictures or maps, please do let us know. If you have noticed any errors or outdated facts, or have suggestions for places to include on the routes, we would be delighted to hear from you. Please drop us an email at hello@insightguides.com. Thanks!

CREDITS

Explore Lisbon
Editor: Sarah Clark
Author: Susie Boulton
Head of Production: Rebeka Davies
Picture Editor: Tom Smyth
Cartography: original cartography Carte
Photo credits: Alamy 35, 136; AWL Images 92/93; Bigstock 67; Design Hotels 106ML, 108; Four Seasons Hotels 106MC, 110, 111; Getty Images 4/5T, 8/9T, 26/27T, 39, 43, 50, 56/57, 62/63, 74, 75, 76T, 116/117, 119, 122/123; Heritage Lisbon Hotels 106MR, 106ML; Heritage Lisbon Hotels/Telmo Miller 114; imageBROKER/REX/Shutterstock 96; iStock 7M, 26MC, 26MR, 38, 40, 41L, 51L, 59, 61, 70, 71B, 81L, 83L, 84, 91, 100B, 120, 134; Leonardo 106MC, 106MR, 106/107T, 109, 112, 115; Lydia Evans/Apa Publications 1, 6TL, 6ML, 6BC, 6/7T, 7MR, 7MR, 8ML, 8MC, 8MR, 8MR, 10, 11L, 10/11, 12, 12/13, 16, 17L, 16/17, 18, 18/19, 20, 21L, 20/21, 22, 22/23, 26MR, 26ML, 30, 31L, 30/31, 32, 32/33, 34, 40/41, 42, 44, 44/45, 46, 47L, 46/47, 48, 48/49, 52, 58, 65L, 64/65, 70/71T, 76/77, 80B, 80T, 82B, 84/85, 86, 86/87, 88T, 88B, 89L, 88/89, 90, 94, 96/97, 104/105M, 118, 120/121, 124, 124/125, 126, 126/127, 128, 128/129, 130, 130/131, 132, 132/133, 134/135; Palmstar Media/Cinemate/REX/Shutterstock 137; PortoBay Hotels & Resorts 113; Public domain 24, 25, 52/53; Shutterstock 6MC, 14/15, 28/29, 36/37, 50/51, 54, 55, 56, 60, 64, 66, 68/69, 72/73, 76B, 78/79, 80/81, 82T, 82/83, 95L, 94/95, 98/99, 100T, 102B, 102T, 103, 104, 105T, 104/105T; SuperStock 53L, 57L, 101; Turismo de Lisboa 4ML, 4MC, 4MR, 4MR, 4MC, 4ML, 8ML, 8MC, 26ML, 26MC
Cover credits: Shutterstock (main&bottom)

Printed by CTPS – China
All Rights Reserved
© 2017 Apa Digital (CH) AG and
Apa Publications (UK) Ltd

First Edition 2017

No part of this book may be reproduced, stored in a retrieval system or transmitted in any form or means electronic, mechanical, photocopying, recording or otherwise, without prior written permission from Apa Publications.

Every effort has been made to provide accurate information in this publication, but changes are inevitable. The publisher cannot be responsible for any resulting loss, inconvenience or injury.

DISTRIBUTION

UK, Ireland and Europe
Apa Publications (UK) Ltd
sales@insightguides.com
United States and Canada
Ingram Publisher Services
ips@ingramcontent.com
Australia and New Zealand
Woodslane
info@woodslane.com.au
Southeast Asia
Apa Publications (Singapore) Pte
singaporeoffice@insightguides.com
Hong Kong, Taiwan and China
Apa Publications (HK) Ltd
hongkongoffice@insightguides.com
Worldwide
Apa Publications (UK) Ltd
sales@insightguides.com

SPECIAL SALES, CONTENT LICENSING AND COPUBLISHING

Insight Guides can be purchased in bulk quantities at discounted prices. We can create special editions, personalised jackets and corporate imprints tailored to your needs.
sales@insightguides.com
www.insightguides.biz

INDEX